BOSNIA ✦ In the Footsteps of Gavrilo Princip

The University of Alberta Press

BOSNIA

In the Footsteps of Gavrilo Princip

TONY FABIJANČIĆ

Published by
The University of Alberta Press
Ring House 2
Edmonton, Alberta, Canada T6G 2E1

LIBRARY AND ARCHIVES CANADA CATALOGUING IN PUBLICATION

Fabijančić, Tony, 1966–
    Bosnia : in the footsteps of Gavrilo Princip / Tony Fabijančić.

Includes index.
ISBN 978-0-88864-51-7

    1. Princip, Gavrilo, 1894–1918. 2. Franz Ferdinand, Archduke of Austria, 1863–1914—
Assassination. 3. Bosnia and Herzegovina—History. 4. Nationalism—Yugoslavia.
5. Assassins—Bosnia and Herzegovina—Biography. 6. Serbs—Bosnia and Herzegovina—
Biography. 7. Fabijančić, Tony, 1966– —Travel—Bosnia and Herzegovina. 8. Bosnia and
Herzegovina—Description and travel. I. Title.

DR1728.P75F32 2009   949.742   C2009-902154-4

The University of Alberta Press is committed to protecting our natural environment. As part of our
efforts, this book is printed on Enviro Paper: it contains 100% post-consumer recycled fibres and is
acid- and chlorine-free.

The University of Alberta Press gratefully acknowledges the support received for its publishing
program from The Canada Council for the Arts. The University of Alberta Press also gratefully
acknowledges the financial support of the Government of Canada through the Book Publishing
Industry Development Program (BPIDP) and from the Alberta Foundation for the Arts for its publishing activities.

Photo of Belgrade on pages 52–53 is courtesy of European Commission,
http://ec.europa.eu/enlargement/press_corner/photo_gallery/serbia_en.htm

✦ CONTENTS

✦ AUTHOR'S NOTE

I HAVE ANGLICIZED some spellings because they are familiar to English speakers (Yugoslavia, not *Jugoslavija*; Belgrade, not
Beograd). As I use them, the nouns "Serb" and "Croat" denote
individuals, and "Serbian" and "Croatian" denote languages, lin-
guistic issues, matters of state, or serve as adjectives. Rather than
the term "Bosniak," which has been prevalent since the war in the
1990s, I preferred "Bosnian Muslim" for its familiarity among general readers. Words in languages other than English are italicized
and English rules of capitalization of foreign terms are followed
throughout unless they appear otherwise in citations (*Narodna
Odbrana*, not *Narodna odbrana*). For concision, "Bosnia-Herzegovina"
is often shortened to "Bosnia," though in Chapter 6 Herzegovina
is treated as a separate entity. All photographs are mine, unless
otherwise indicated.

Serbo-Croatian letters used in this book (with pronunciations) are listed below:

c—*ts*, as in ca*ts*
č—*ch*, as in *ch*ur*ch*
ć—like *ch*, but softer, as in future
đ—*dj*, as in *j*ungle
ј—*y*, as in *y*esterday
š—*sh*, as in *sh*ip
ž—*zh*, as in treasure

✦ PREFACE

IT WAS WHILE RESEARCHING another work—a historical fiction set in Bosnia-Herzegovina's deep past—that the idea came to me to follow the path of the infamous assassin who set the First World War in motion with his shots on June 28, 1914.

After finishing my first travel book about Croatia, I decided to continue with the complicated, ethnically fraught, former Yugoslavia as the main focus of my writing, partly out of fascination with the place, its people, and its history, and partly because I started to sense a much bigger project emerge, like a shape under the ocean's surface. I imagined that Yugoslavia—or, to use a broader, more complicated term, the Balkans—could potentially absorb some of my former academic interests: the importance of space in its different facets, an analysis of modernity, and the mentality of the rural outsider. At the same time, I thought that focusing on the Balkans would allow me to get out into the "field" and write in a more creative, non-scholarly form.

So far, you might say, so good. But around that time, to supplement my knowledge of Bosnia-Herzegovina, I read Vladimir Dedijer's *The Road to Sarajevo*, a history of the assassination of Archduke Franz Ferdinand from the Bosnian perspective. The book shattered my preconceptions about the country and the assassination. *The Road to Sarajevo* is not just a great historical work, meticulously researched and relentlessly factual, but a work of great *literary* skill, too—carefully narrated and emotionally powerful. It begins with the assassination itself, which causes our sympathies to lie with the victims, but slowly, almost imperceptibly, it builds a different truth out of historical, cultural, political, economical, and personal information. Even though *The Road to Sarajevo* has its weaknesses, it convincingly recasts Gavrilo Princip's identity for me, a sign of the book's spell.

My Croatian friend Neven Kralj wondered about this new interest of mine, asking me what I *really* thought about Gavrilo Princip. With this question he got to the heart of a problem that dogged me throughout this project. Why should a Canadian of Croatian background be interested in writing about a Serbian hero? My answer to Neven is best appreciated by reading this book in its entirety, but it can be summed up thus: because the assassination of Franz Ferdinand is a *significant* event in Bosnian and world history (as opposed to a *good* or *bad* one), because it is another supposed expression of extreme Serbian nationalism in the eyes of many Bosnians, and, maybe most important, because it is a gripping story with a fascinating cast of characters, it serves as an excellent frame for a travel book about Bosnia-Herzegovina. Rather than sympathizing with Princip, the *Serb* assassin, I saw narrative potential in Princip, the *symbol*.

But my interest in Princip went deeper than I was letting on. In truth, not only had I become fascinated with the events that led up to the assassination, as well as the personalities of the assassins themselves, but I had also come to understand these young men in a profound way, to walk step by step with them, and even to admire them for their convictions and, in some cases, their bravery. I saw more than narrative potential in Princip; I supported and empathized with this naïve, idealistic son of poor Bosnian peasants who believed he had struck a blow for his people.

The reason I felt as I did was shrouded in mystery, even to myself. There are, after all, less controversial historical figures I could have written about. Perhaps my tendency to back the underdog, which has been evident since my boyhood, was at the back of it. In any case, I felt I had been entrusted with a story that people no longer knew in truth, if they ever did, but that I felt they ought to know. In time, partly as a result of travelling through Bosnia-Herzegovina, my views about the assassination grew more complex, and my kinship with the assassins became more troubled.

Early on, however, the reality of the country itself had yet to impact my views on the assassination. Mine was a mainly theoretical knowledge. Besides Dedijer's book, I poured over hundreds of obscure sources, had my wife translate numerous works in Cyrillic, had long conversations with her and other members of my family, and in general lived and breathed many of my waking hours in 1914. I imagined crucial moments in the lives of the assassins, reconstructing the scenes, conversations, and atmosphere. For example, again and again I visited the room where Danilo Ilić and Gavrilo Princip spent hours arguing over the value of the assassination, and I felt the tension between them as Ilić's cautious reasoning foundered against the relentless will of his former protegé. I thought I had it in me to recreate such moments, the subtle human interactions, the gaps and silences of history. For a while, I toyed with the idea of writing a historical novel, but eventually I concluded that a travelogue would be the best approach, since no one had ever written about 1914 in this way, and also because my talents as a writer and researcher seem to work best in travel narratives.

But even had I explained all this to Neven, he would have had other doubts about my project. "In dees moment of speaking, I think you take too big job. Bosnia is very complex, and you will fail."

True, writing about Bosnia-Herzegovina was daunting; its multi-ethnic and religious character (Greek Orthodox Serbs, Muslims, and Catholic Croats) makes its labyrinthine history especially complicated. But my intention was never to tell Bosnia's whole story, only to open a window onto one aspect of its past and character. So I ignored Neven's warnings and pressed ahead.

The choice of the travel genre to retell the story of Sarajevo, 1914, has the advantage of being commensurate with the lives of the Bosnian assassins. Most were wanderers who walked to the far ends of their country and back, went to Serbia and elsewhere in search of education, work, military glory, and revolution. They crossed geographical borders and also social ones (being on the edges, on the margins of society). When Vaso Čubrilović described Princip as a *stuha*, "a slightly satiric designation, signifying a restless spirit, who could never settle down, always wishing to roam around," he could have been describing most of the other assassins as well.[1] Indeed, the history of Bosnia-Herzegovina is one of movement, from the transhumant Vlachs, who eventually settled in border territory between the Ottoman and Habsburgian Empires, to *Hajduci*, who practiced banditry in the narrow passages of the Dinaric Alps, and to countless wanderers, such as Gypsies, peddlers, masons, thieves, tinkers, and bards.

But one problem with travel writing was that as I tried to give life to inert facts and landscapes, I opened myself up to the accusation of inaccurately depicting or romanticizing people and events long lost to time (precisely the shortcoming I had found in fiction). How can a visit to a prison cell over ninety years after Princip was there tell you anything about him? The short answer is: it cannot. The longer answer is that it can help establish the physical conditions of the place as it might have appeared in 1914, its more inaccessible ambience and, *potentially*, the nature of the doomed soul of the man who spent his last years there. Going to Theresienstadt was one occasion among many to peel away history's layers.

As the weeks went by, though, I knew the story I was telling was not only about the past but about the present, as well. In writing history, I was coming away with pictures of contemporary Bosnia, too, so I arrived at the decision to use the events of 1914 as a window onto the new Bosnia that emerged from the violent chaos of the 1990s. Gavrilo Princip in this new schema became a barometer for ethnic relations today. Ask the Serbs what they think of Princip and you will get a very different answer than if you ask a Bosnian Croat or Muslim.

My travel itinerary was loosely that of Princip's life: from his place of origin in the Krajina to Sarajevo, where he received part of his education, then east to Serbia, and back to Sarajevo, where he assassinated Franz Ferdinand. But I also went elsewhere to cover some important moments—through eastern Bosnia, where the assassins journeyed clandestinely with revolvers and bombs; to Doboj and Tuzla, where Danilo Ilić picked up the arms from Miško Jovanović; and also to Mostar in Herzegovina, where the political and intellectual life of students was especially vibrant, and where widespread student unrest had erupted before the assassination.

A warning to readers: the book I've written isn't a scholarly work in which every historical figure, event, or issue is treated exhaustively or systematically. Instead I attempted to tell the "true" story of the assassination and contemporary Bosnia-Herzegovina more impressionistically. In doing so, my chance experiences on the road and the beauties of the landscape also find a place in the book, as I shadowed the ghost of Gavrilo Princip.

✦ ACKNOWLEDGEMENTS

I WOULD LIKE TO THANK all those at the University of Alberta Press, whose long hours and expert vision greatly improved this book. My thanks especially to Michael Luski, former acquistions editor at the University of Alberta Press, for his interest in this project long before it took shape, his steady advice over the years, and his thoroughness as an editor. Earlier versions of some chapters have appeared in the *Globe and Mail* and the *Toronto Star*. My thanks to the editors.

I owe a debt to Josip Fabijančić, my father, for travelling with me through much of Bosnia-Herzegovina. These were our last trips together researching a project of mine, so they have a fond place in my memory, even if they weren't always enjoyable at the time! My wife, Tea, took care of our kids while I was off on this adventure, expertly translated various Serbo-Croatian texts in Cyrillic, and offered excellent advice on the manuscript's style.

My mother, Ursula, proofread the manuscript with her usual rigour; any stylistic problems are entirely my own. Thank you to my sister, Natasha, for going over the introduction.

I am thankful to Memorial University for funds supporting this project.

Finally, I am indebted to the people of Bosnia-Herzegovina, especially those whom I obliged to recall deeply painful memories of the war.

✦ INTRODUCTION ✦ HISTORICAL BACKGROUND

THE ASSASSINATION of Archduke Franz Ferdinand von Österreich-Este, heir apparent to the Habsburg Empire, on June 28, 1914, was the catalyst for the First World War. Because the assassin was a Bosnian Serb, whose weapons were procured from the Serbian state arsenal at Kragujevac, the assassination was a perfect pretext for Austrian hawks in the Austro-Hungarian war cabinet to crush a Serbian state that had become emboldened, although weakened, after its victories during the Balkan Wars. Despite evidence that the Serbian government had not planned the assassination, Austria-Hungary issued Serbia an ultimatum, a disingenuous document designed to be rejected since it demanded, among other things, that Austrian delegates lead a judicial investigation into the assassination on Serbian soil. Because Serbia demurred on this demand on the grounds that it violated its constitution, Austria-Hungary declared war,

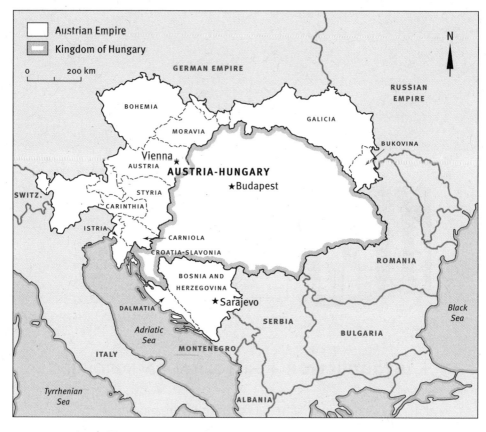

1914 Austria-Hungary.

embroiling Europe in the bloodiest conflict the world had seen
to that point. By 1918 over ten million had died; the Habsburg,
Hohenzollern, Romanov, and Ottoman empires had collapsed;
and the face of Europe had changed forever.

The seeds for the assassination of Franz Ferdinand were sown
in the nineteenth century with the rise of nationalism among the
South Slavs, which came to a head with the outright annexation
of Bosnia-Herzegovina by Austria-Hungary in 1908.[1] Although
the Austrians wanted to limit Serbia's economic independence
and ever more blatant nationalism, especially as it pertained to
Bosnia, a main result of the annexation was that it made many

more ethnic Serbs Habsburg subjects and, more than any other event, sparked in Serbs and Croats ambitions to carve out independent states or unite in a South Slavic federation, to be known as Yugoslavia. The annexation also led to the rise in 1911 of a radical Serbian militarist group called *Ujedinjenje ili Smrt* (Union or Death),[2] popularly known as the Black Hand, which set up a secret revolutionary network in Serbia and Bosnia, and which provided the assassins with the weapons for the assassination.

The two men who met fatefully on June 28, 1914, embodied the conflict between the Austro-Hungarian Empire and its Bosnian-Serb subjects. Franz Ferdinand, nephew of Emperor Franz Joseph, was born in Graz on December 18, 1863, and until his death lived a mostly comfortable life that befitted his aristocratic station, though he was not without his troubles, having survived a bout of tuberculosis (the disease, which, ironically, took Princip's life in Theresienstadt). Ferdinand's luck held, though, and he was chosen heir apparent after the three leading candidates died prematurely—one before a Mexican firing squad, the second (the emperor's son) from a self-inflicted gunshot, and the third from typhoid after he ignored advice and drank from the river Jordan during a pilgrimage to Jerusalem.[3]

Ferdinand's explosive temperament, erratic tendencies, unwavering prejudices, stubbornness, and thin skin did not make him an ideal leader of a complex, multi-ethnic empire. As one historian put it, he was "overbearing and hot-tempered, and was prone to fits of ungovernable rage. At shooting parties he would sometimes blaze away at everything within range, terrorizing all his companions. He is known on one occasion to have drawn his sword and hacked furiously at the upholstery in his railroad compartment because of some incident that displeased him. Certainly there was much speculation in court circles concerning his mental health, particularly because of the history of insanity in his family."[4]

Ferdinand's known hatred for the Hungarians, Austria's ruling partners, did not bode well for future relations in the empire.

*Franz Ferdinand
in uniform.*

[from Dedijer, Sarajevo 1914,
p. 951]

It was bad taste on their part ever to have come to Europe, he once complained. Besides his dislike for the Hungarians, he did not seem especially fond of any of his future subjects, and he was also an unrepentant anti-Semite. If he did not love the people, however, he certainly loved to hunt. By 1897, at age thirty-three, he had shot his thousandth stag, and by 1910 his five thousandth. It is ironic that a man who enjoyed hunting so much would end up being hunted down and shot to death himself.

Signs of the archduke's gentler side included an interest in art (though limited mainly to objets d'art of St. George and the dragon), his fostering of a model farm and collection of roses at his estate in Bohemia, and his love for his wife, Countess Sophie Chotek von Chotkowa und Wognin, who had been born into a poor family of the lower Czech aristocracy.[5] Against the wishes of the emperor, Ferdinand insisted on marrying her and was eventually granted permission for a morganatic marriage. This meant he could retain the throne but had to forego his children's rights of inheritance. Ferdinand's loyalty to Sophie Chotek came with yet another price; the couple was not permitted to appear in public side by side, due to Habsburg protocol. But the stinging embarrassment of these rebukes was suspended temporarily with the couple's trip to Bosnia-Herzegovina, where for the first time they were seen together on official occasions. The assassination occurred on the fourteenth anniversary of Ferdinand's morganatic oath, which also happened to fall on the anniversary of the Battle of Kosovo in 1389, which pitted the Ottoman Turks against a Serb-led army, and that was forever marked in Serbian national mythology as a catastrophic defeat.

Why was Franz Ferdinand a target in Bosnia-Herzegovina? The most obvious answer is that he was a top personage of hated Austria-Hungary. For the young assassins, ridding Bosnia-Herzegovina of the future heir was a step toward political liberation. In addition, Ferdinand was a target because of his reputed designs on Serbia, which had leaked into the popular Serbian imagination through anti-Habsburg propaganda.[6] But Ferdinand may never have had such expansionist intentions, if we are to believe his own misgivings about conflict with Serbia. What would it get them, he wondered? A few plum trees, and many more thieves, murderers, and crooks. He had, however, dabbled with the idea of trialism, the formation of a third, South Slavic unit within the Austro-Hungarian Empire. Ferdinand understood that some form of reorganization of the empire was critical if it were not to be doomed. But by 1909, he seemed to have rejected trialism as a solution. In a letter to Kaiser Wilhelm II, he called such an eventuality a "misfortune," mainly because it established the conditions for a Slavic empire, spurred on by the rapprochement of Croats and Serbs, which threatened the stability of the empire. He blamed the dangerous ambitions of the Slavs on the "infamous, antidynastic, lying, unreliable" Hungarians, who "achieve everything by revolutionary pressure and blackmail." If only a stop could be put to these "shameless Magyar intrigues (which would be quite easy to do, since the Magyar as a true Hun and Asiatic always boasts but then gives way in the face of energetic action) the Slavs would end their violent onrush and would again submit calmly and quietly to the culturally far superior Germans."[7]

We will never know whether Ferdinand's wariness of open conflict with the Serbs or his autocratic leanings would have won over in the end. Had he lived long enough to rule, he might very well have found himself embroiled in conflict with the Hungarians rather than with the unruly Serbs. Ultimately, Franz Ferdinand was probably as hated by those in the upper echelon of the Austro-Hungarian Empire, both Hungarian and Austrian, as by the man who killed him.

✦ Gavrilo Princip was born in the hamlet of Gornji Obljaj in mountainous, western Bosnia-Herzegovina. On the day of his birth, July 13, 1894, his mother had gathered hay bales in the sun-baked fields, washed clothes in a creek, and milked a cow before she felt labour pains and struggled back to the dark stone house. Her labour was violent and swift, and she had just enough time to lie on the earthen floor by the hearth before the baby was born. Her mother-in-law arrived, bit through the umbilical cord, stoked the fire, and poured *šljivovica* for arriving guests. Despite the odds (six of his nine siblings died in infancy), and the conditions (smoke from the open fire filled the windowless house most of the day), Gavrilo Princip managed to survive.

His parents were poor peasants who lived off the little arable land they owned and the added labour of Princip's father, who took various jobs, including that of mailman. A sinewy, tough, pious man set in the traditional ways of peasant life, he was known to have hoisted a sixty-pound mail bag in the winter

*Gavrilo Princip
at sixteen.*

[from Dedijer, Sarajevo 1914,
p. 951]

months and to have driven his mail cart religiously in poor road
conditions throughout the rest of the year, breaking his leg once
as he reined in his horses on a mountain pass in an effort to save
mail and passengers. His stiff correctness (he neither drank nor
swore) was likely the source of the villagers' ridicule and was off-
set by his wife's liberal spirit. It was because of her that Princip
went to school. Her indifference to religion may have rubbed off
on her son, as well, becoming in him a more extreme, anarchist-
tinged atheism; and the hard life she (and all peasant women)
led shaped his attitudes about the liberation of women from
patriarchal Bosnian society.

The basic parts of Princip's personality showed up early on—
a desire to be alone, an emotional and intellectual sensitivity
that manifested itself in his love of reading, a sense of inferiority

mainly due to his small size, and a tempestuous, explosive side (his mother recalled how "every blow he received he would return twofold"[8]). Some historians have emphasized the importance of Princip's need to compensate for his small stature in his decision to assassinate Ferdinand. He had to perform some act of exceptional bravery, they argue, to prove himself, especially after having been rejected by the Serbian guerrillas during the Balkan Wars.

The rest of Princip's brief life is that of a politicized Bosnian-Serb youth in the last days of the Austro-Hungarian Empire. His road took him first to Sarajevo, where he studied in the Merchants School, and where he was exposed to anarchistic, socialist, and communist writing. Then he went to Serbia on the wave of war enthusiasm during the First Balkan War, spending his days in the restaurants and cafés of Belgrade among an indigent, radicalized Bosnian diaspora. When a newspaper clipping announcing the archduke's decision to visit Bosnia-Herzegovina arrived in Belgrade anonymously, Princip, Čabrinović, and their comrade, Trifko Grabež, came to the decision that he had to be killed.

For the rest of the world, not versed in Yugoslav history, Princip's method of achieving his generation's political goals, the so-called propaganda of the deed, which in retrospect seems so rash, ruthless, and ultimately unsuccessful, assures his infamy. Across Bosnia-Herzegovina, though, the assassination has always had its supporters, and Princip has always been a more complex figure here than he is elsewhere in the world. Since 1914 he has assumed various identities: that of an anti-Habsburg revolutionary hero, a martyr for Bosnian nationhood, a naïve adolescent with noble ideals, a Serbian nationalist, and, since the bloody course of the war in the 1990s, if not before, a Serbian terrorist (at least from the point of view of Bosnian Croats and Muslims).

Gavrilo Princip's own choice for an identity was that of "Yugoslav nationalist" (in Serbo-Croatian "Yugoslav" means "South Slav"). However, Princip went on to complicate the

Bosnia-Herzegovina today.

straightforward idealism of South Slavic egalitarianism when he said at the trial: "It was understood that Serbia as the free part of the South Slavs had the moral duty to help with the unification, to be to the South Slavs as the Piedmont was to Italy."[9] This concept of the Serbs' moral duty to guide the other South Slavs enjoyed its heyday at the start of the twentieth century, when even Croats genuinely looked east for leadership in the wake of Serbia's successes in the Balkan Wars.[10] That was still a moment when

Yugoslavia was an imaginary nation untainted by the realities of the first royal Yugoslav dictatorship, Tito's purges, and the ethnic cleansing of the 1990s.[11] But many Bosnian Croats and Muslims in 1914 clearly considered Princip a purely Serbian nationalist rather than a fiercely determined idealist guided by the shining principles of South Slavic unity (as the socialist Yugoslav government would depict him later).

What does all this matter to present-day Bosnia-Herzegovina? After all, the war is over, Yugoslavia is dead, and Gavrilo Princip has been mainly forgotten by Bosnians eager to leave the traumatic past behind and get on with the peaceful present. One reason Princip continues to be important is because he remains a gauge for ethnic tensions that have surrounded Serbian irredentist hopes, tensions that lie dormant but unresolved. For many Bosnians today, the ethno-nationalistic motivations of Gavrilo Princip were also at the heart of the war in the 1990s. The historical accuracy of this conclusion can be debated, of course, but it is clear is that the nature of Princip's existence within the latent memory of Bosnians, the manner in which his identity and motivations are interpreted today, reveals something about Bosnia's ethnic terrain.[12]

This leads me to another reason for revisiting Gavrilo Princip and the assassination of 1914 in a travel book about Bosnia. Because of Bosnia's reputation as an inherently violent place, filled with "ancient ethnic hatreds," it finds itself squarely situated within the ambit of the Balkans, which have acquired derogatory qualities in the West's wider social imagination.[13] Princip's act is the "great crime of the Balkans,...indeed their original sin."[14] As such, it has contributed fundamentally in binding up a geographic term, the "Balkans," with negative cultural, political, social, and ideological overtones. Western commentators often mention the assassination when they want to demean the region. "It is an intolerable affront to human and political nature," wrote one, "that these wretched and unhappy little countries in the Balkan peninsula can, and do, have quarrels that cause world wars. Some hundred and fifty thousand young Americans died because of an event in a mud-caked, primitive village, Sarajevo. Loathsome and almost obscure snarls in Balkan politics, hardly intelligible to a western reader, are still vital to the peace of Europe, and perhaps the world."[15] Whether I wanted to or not, by following in the footsteps of Princip, I was also entering that debate about the correctness or incorrectness of Bosnia's inclusion in the "barbaric" Balkans.[16]

✦ CHRONOLOGY

600–800	Arrival of Slavs in the Balkans
1389	Battle between Ottoman and Christian forces in Kosovo
1463	Ottoman conquest of Bosnia
1683	Failed Ottoman assault on Vienna
1804	First Serbian uprising
1815	Second Serbian uprising
1863	Birth of Franz Ferdinand
1875	Peasant uprising in Herzegovina
1878	Treaty of Berlin; Austro-Hungarian occupation of Bosnia-Herzegovina
1894	Birth of Gavrilo Princip
1903	Assassination of Alexander Obrenović and wife
1908	Austro-Hungarian annexation of Bosnia-Herzegovina; *Narodna Odbrana* founded

1909	Zagreb Treason Trials
1911	*Ujedinjenje ili Smrt (Crna Ruka)* founded
1912	First Balkan War; assassination attempt by Bogdan Žerajić against governor of Bosnia, General Marijan Varešanin
1913	Second Balkan War
1914	Assassination of Franz Ferdinand by Gavrilo Princip
1914–1918	First World War
1918	Death of Gavrilo Princip; Kingdom of Serbs, Croats, and Slovenes founded
1929	First state of Yugoslavia founded
1939–1945	Second World War
1945	Second state of Yugoslavia founded
1980	Death of Tito
1986	Memorandum of the Serbian Academy of Arts and Sciences
1990	Ethnic discord in the Krajina
1990–1991	Fighting in Slovenia and Croatia
1991	Croatia and Slovenia declare independence from Yugoslavia
1992	Bosnia-Herzegovina declares independence from Yugoslavia
1992–1995	War in Bosnia-Herzegovina
1995	Dayton Peace Agreement
1999	War in Kosovo between NATO and Serbia
2006	Montenegro declares independence from Serbian coalition

1 ✦ THE KRAJINA

✦ BACK TO ORIGINS

I WENT FIRST in search of Gavrilo Princip's roots in the hamlet
of Gornji Obljaj. After two years of research, during which I travelled to Bosnia in my imagination almost daily, breathing in
the atmosphere of 1914, I was eager to step onto Bosnian soil and
finally begin seeking out traces of Princip's presence. Although no
one in my family shared my obsession with the assassination, I
didn't travel alone on the first stage of my journey. I was accompanied by my father, a trustworthy companion, but also a reluctant
traveller to Bosnia, who had inherited most of the Croats' prejudices about the country—that it was backward, unstable, and
in the main not worth visiting. Nevertheless, he agreed to come
along to take photos, help read maps, and keep me out of trouble.
My wife came up with this last duty because she thought I'd tested
luck once too often on my solitary trips. She also claimed, based
on slim evidence, that I always got into fights.

1

"Remember the security guy who choked you when you wouldn't give up the hotel's beach mat?"

"Why should I have paid? It was seven in the morning and there wasn't anyone there!" I retorted.

"Or the fisherman you angered when you asked if that boat was his? You can be rude, not to mention annoying, asking people questions out of the blue. Something could happen to you travelling all by yourself."

Friends of mine in Croatia had echoed her worries, not about my rudeness getting me into trouble, but about the dangers I might encounter on the road. When they spoke about Bosnia these otherwise intelligent, reasonable, and cosmopolitan people sounded slightly irrational and hysterical. My second cousin, an anaesthesiologist at a heart surgery clinic in Krapina, warned me against going altogether.

"You do not know what you will find. You drive into a small place and you want to talk to someone. Maybe you meet a man. He is crazy still from war, and he is desperate. There is no job, no future in such small places. You can just disappear."

Just disappear! This ominous phrase stayed with me throughout the winter before my trip, working on my imagination and causing me to picture disturbing scenes in the "small places" I would have to visit.

Nevertheless, in June 2005, father in tow, I drove south from Croatia's capital, Zagreb, and into the Krajina district, the mountainous borderland between northwestern Bosnia-Herzegovina and central Croatia. In 1990, ethnic conflict in this region where Princip was born contributed crucially to the rapid collapse of Yugoslavia as descendants of Orthodox settlers set up roadblocks on the Croatian side to protest what they deemed to be their increasingly precarious position in a nationalist Croatia. Mockingly dubbed the "log revolution" by Croats, this event in Knin began a process of secession that resulted in the founding of a self-proclaimed Serbian statelet within Croatia—the Serbian Republic of Krajina.[1]

How did things stand now, I wondered? The road between Karlovac and the Bosnian border at Maljevac wound through hilly farming country, where almost every house was abandoned or destroyed, where vineyards had reverted to nature and fruit orchards were untended. To my mind this lonely place was the legacy of the Krajina Serbs. I expected much the same on the Bosnian side.

At the border crossing, a young guard in a neatly pressed uniform demanded all our documents, including our drivers' licences and car rental agreement, and proceeded to pour over them in his shack. Through the window I could see him hold our passports up in the air then examine them under a scanner, while his partner jotted notes in a big black book. My driver's licence seemed to give them the most trouble, and they held it up to the light then bent down to look at it under a magnifying glass, before asking me to explain a word at the top.

"Newfoundland," I said. "It's a province in Canada. KANADA," I repeated slowly.

He looked at me skeptically then retreated to his booth to confer with his partner. They huddled together, passing the card back and forth. One of them picked up the phone to ask someone for advice. Finally, they entered something down in their book, passed back our documents and waved us through. The episode had lasted ten minutes, and the guy behind us, evidently used to such delays, had gotten out of his car to have a smoke.

"Same old shit," my father said as we drove off.

"What do you mean?"

"Nothing's changed since communism. The country is new but the techniques are still the same."

"Didn't you used to have problems at the Yugoslav border?" I asked.

"They liked to make us wait."

"Those of you who were coming back, who had left."

"That's right."

"Were the border guards Serbs?"

"That's right."

"Who were these guys?" I wondered.

"They were Muslims."

"How are you so sure?"

"Listen," he answered, drawing out the word and giving me a dry smile as he did when he was certain about something. "I can tell. They were Muslims. No question."

"They go to a lot of trouble here, don't they," I said.

"They have high standards in Bosnia," he cackled. "They don't just let anyone in."

We drove at a leisurely pace through hilly farm country, which was disrupted occasionally by outcroppings of rocks as in the Dalmatian hinterland. To my surprise, there was life in this part of the new Muslim-Croatian Federation of Bosnia. Everywhere I looked there were new businesses, newly façaded farmhouses, corn and wheat fields, and cropped meadows with skinny hay ricks like the minarets of mosques. In Velika Kladuša, a Muslim city in what used to be mainly Serbian territory, hundreds of school kids were out for lunch, the cafés were full, and groups of pretty girls walked arm in arm on the crowded sidewalks. A tall, curvy woman in spandex tights and black pumps crossed the street and swayed her pink haunches invitingly in front of us. Coming the other way, like a contrary position in an argument, were two teenaged girls in black hijabs. Their stiff formality stuck out from the secular Muslim crowd, reminding me of Harry De Windt's "uncanny" encounter with similar "sable-clad forms flitting silently through the streets" of Mostar in 1907.[2]

It was noon. The wavery call to prayer floated from the speaker on the white minaret of the mosque. The thin voice hung for a while in the hot air, an exotic sound to my ears. Up to now, my research had focused mainly on the Serbs, the main players in the assassination, so I had forgotten a little that Bosnia was in large part a Muslim country—that the Muslims, second in numbers to the Serbs in Princip's time, had become the majority.[3] As the muezzin's call faded from hearing, I took a look around, still transfixed. Though the hot streets were jammed with people, only two men kicked off their sandals and stepped inside.

"You can't expect people to go five times a day, can you?!" shrugged Sejat Mohammedabdić, a gas attendant we met out of town. We were sitting in the gas station's makeshift café having a drink before we moved on to Bihać. He was telling us that the Muslims of Bosnia weren't especially devout, despite the new religious climate since the war. He said the girls in hijabs probably belonged to one of the sects that showed up in the 1990s. "Mostly outsiders, from other Muslim states." It was ironic, he thought, that Serbian propaganda in the 1990's about the dangers of Muslim extremism in Bosnia had probably intensified fundamentalism instead of eradicating it.

Despite his comments, Sejat didn't seem interested in railing against the Serbs. Maybe he was fed up with politics, or maybe he was wary of opening up to us. I dropped the subject and told him instead about the woman in the pink tights. He laughed. "Too bad you left so soon. She could've done you a favour!" My father laughed, too. He had found something in common with this Bosnian Muslim. Earlier, he had treaded sprightly behind the lady in question, a little too close for my liking, reached out his hands and pretended to squeeze her rear. It was a gesture Sejat would have appreciated.

When we were about to leave, Sejat waved across the road. "My house," he said, "is your house."

We thanked him and drove on. Having been on the road since morning we decided to have lunch in a village near Bihać. On a curve of the village's only street, the main road itself, we got out of the car and approached a man sitting on a stool behind a small wooden kiosk. Sliding glass doors protected chunks of roast lamb from the flies, and on a chopping board were two knives and a hatchet. When I asked the vendor, a thin, hooked-nose fellow, whether anything came with the meat, he said no and suggested without hesitation that we eat at the restaurant next door. This we did, somewhat guiltily, as the lamb seller continued to wait for customers, looking bored, rubbing his eyes and watching the girls go by.

I ate veal shish kebabs (ražnići) and fries served with a spicy condiment called ajvar, made of tomatoes, onions, and eggplant. Undulating music from the radio took me back to my childhood summers in Croatia, when it was still part of Yugoslavia and where Bosnian music could be heard from time to time. This folk music with its sinewy lead vocals, set to a modern electronic beat, was pervasive in Bosnia and reminded me again of the longstanding eastern Balkan and Ottoman influences in the country. When I finished eating, I descended the steep steps to the washroom and stood gingerly on the treads of the ceramic toilet. The light in the washroom didn't work, but I noticed that in the corner beside the toilet was a one-litre version of the mineral water I had drunk with my meal. It wasn't filled with mineral water any longer, but ordinary tap water, and served another purpose altogether.

We headed east along the turquoise Una River that winds through deep valleys cleft into steep hills of oak and fir. On small beaches were wooden huts, kayaks, and boys jumping into the river. Farther on we saw a castle on top of a mountain, its Bohemian-looking spires an anomaly in this part of Muslim Bosnia. Soon after, we passed through the city of Bihać, the capital of the so-called Bihać pocket.

It was here that internecine dissension between local Muslims and their federal counterparts turned into outright fighting in the 1990s. This division was due to the secessionist intentions of Fikret Abdić, a privateer accused of co-operating with both Bosnian Serbs and Croats. Abdić turned the Bihać pocket into "one enormous black market," which provided food, clothes, and drink to its mainly Muslim inhabitants.[4] He appeared inspired by the legendary Muslim guerrilla leader in the Second World War, Hussein (Huska) Miljković, whose "Huskina-Krajina" was independent of both the Croat fascists, the *Ustaše*, and the Serb-dominated Partisans. Although Huska couldn't always control his own forces, he ensured the survival of his statelet by co-operating with everybody, especially in trade.[5]

Co-operation between the ethnic groups in the Bihać area, combined with their sense of independence, was evident later, as well. In 1954, the only peasant revolt recorded in postwar Eastern Europe took place here as Serbs, Croats, and Muslims banded together. The communist regime brutally suppressed the rebellion, but locals still remember it. Maybe this memory is one of the reasons Sejat didn't have too much negative to say about his Serbian neighbours.

✦ After leaving Bihać behind, we came eventually to Lipo, a long broad valley bordered by the low wooded spurs of the Dinaric Alps, which thunder southward to Albania. Here I was given a foretaste of Gavrilo Princip's birthplace. There is open space in Lipo, forlorn empty houses backed up against the hills, and abundant pastureland. In these vast corridors, where somber crags tear at the sky and lonely grey stones poke from the grass like menhirs, not a soul was to be seen.

Finally, off the main road, at the end of a dusty trail past an abandoned farmhouse and a little cemetery, we met a young shepherd tending his flock. Damir Peršen, a Croat, was carrying on a traditional practice that Princip and his family had, as well. Damir was eighteen, had a wide face with high cheekbones, and wore a greasy ski jacket and rubber boots (though by then it was a warm sunny afternoon).

My father asked him if he ever got any company out here. A little ruefully, he answered, "No, just the company of wolves. Two came out of the mountains yesterday morning."

Damir Peršen, a Croatian shepherd in the Krajina.

"I hope you have a gun."

"My gun is my best friend," he joked, but with barely the trace of a smile. His eyes kept darting behind us. Like Sejat, Damir seemed a touch uncertain about our presence there. Could he be worried about his safety? Or his sheep? I noticed how our car, parked below us at the end of the stone path, seemed to cut him off from the main road. At that moment he strode forward aggressively and waved a switch of black bark at us. I flinched and turned and saw three wild-looking sheep dogs that had crept up on their bellies. The look in their quiet eyes, the hair up on their necks, made me realize that Damir had actually been more concerned for us than for himself.

After driving the dogs back, he told us he'd been in Lipo since April, one week on and one week off. The sheet of canvas draped across a rope at the edge of a clutch of trees would be his home here until October, when the owner would transport his sheep to Drvar.

Although Serbs continued to live in Drvar, Damir said, those who had once called Lipo home had fled. No one remained except for two old women who lived alone in the woods nearby. Maybe they were the only visitors to the Serbian cemetery we had passed on the way up. All the people buried here, I noticed, died before 1995, the year the Croats retook Krajina.

Between the rickety iron crosses and expensive grey granite headstones engraved with portraits and names of the dead, tall wild grass swayed and whispered. The sun shone and crickets chirped around me. As I listened to the receding bells of Damir's sheep, I reflected on the special character of death here; with no one left to mourn and to show respect, the final fate of most of the dead—to be forgotten by the living—was already taking place in Lipo.

✦ We were getting close to Princip's birthplace. A Serb we met outside Drvar, sitting on his stoop by the road, told us the old house had been turned into a museum. There might be photographs I hadn't seen before, maybe artifacts. I was surprised to learn of the museum and was eager to see this bit of world history.

The hamlet of Gornji Obljaj is located in a desolate region on the northern side of the Dinaric Alps, which divide Bosnia from Croatia's Dalmatian coast. Known as the Krajina, the region was formerly a military border established by the Habsburgs in the sixteenth century, and populated mainly by pastoral Vlachs of the Serbian empire and later by other Christians, mostly Orthodox refugees from the Ottoman Empire who had been invited in by the Austrians, given land, and released from feudal obligations in payment for military service.[6] This military tradition continued on into the nineteenth century, as the valley of Grahovo where Princip was born was maintained as a quasi-military frontier called a *kapetanija*, whose leaders were Bosnian-Muslim feudal lords, a few of whose part-time soldiers were Christians. Some of Princip's ancestors guarded the area against military raids from Austrian and Venetian territory, and against bandits, waiting in the hills to ambush unwanted marauders. Appropriately, the family name before it was changed to "Princip" at the beginning of the nineteenth century was *Čeka*, which means "to wait," as Gavrilo Princip himself did for Franz Ferdinand.

When we entered the valley of Grahovo Polje from the northwest, we saw the pale brown triangle of a mountain far to the east. Gavrilo Princip must have gazed at this peak countless times during the first thirteen years of his life, imagining what lay beyond, before he left for Sarajevo to study in the Merchants School.

From my first moments in this isolated valley, I realized how a mentality would have developed rather differently here than it did in Dalmatia to the south or in central Bosnia to the east. The so-called "Dinaric man" who banded with his family into collectives called *zadruge*, worked the land, and carried a gun, was still around in the nineteenth century. For example, one of Gavrilo Princip's ancestors, Todor Čeka, epitomized the warrior mentality of the Krajina Serbs. A colossal, domineering man, he was the family patriarch and a *matroloz* (border guard) in Ottoman territory who went on business and pleasure sprees over the hills to Dalmatia.

In the rich costumes of his own region, a silver breastplate, a cap with peacocks' feathers, a short musket and a big knife in his cummerbund, he always rode a white horse....When drinking he would go beserk and anyone who came into conflict with him would remember him til his dying day. The story goes that once on the festival of Saint John he was drunk and rode his white stallion through a Catholic village, piercing with his long sharp knife the low straw-roofed huts. He snatched up the most beautiful girl from this Catholic village and kept her at his home for some time....Because of his giant build, his brilliant costume, and the fear he inspired in everybody, the

Moslem beys nicknamed him "Princip." All the members of his family soon changed their old name of Čeka to Princip.[7]

The violent, rebellious spirit of Todor Princip (if not his physique), was passed on to Gavrilo Princip and, many years later, was alive among the Serbs who rebelled against the Croatian government headed by Franjo Tudjman. As Misha Glenny writes, these Serbs, "who did much of the fighting in 1991, are very different from their compatriots in the cities who are known rather frivolously as *Hrbi*, a conflation of *Hrvati* (Croats) and *Srbi* (Serbs). The economic horizons of the rural Serbs are limited, but the early post-feudal concepts of land and home are central to their thinking and sense of security. Passive for decades, when they believed their homes were under threat, their harmless ignorance transformed itself into something very dangerous."[8]

The valley of the Princips could sustain human life, but it was a hard and meagre one for the family. They lacked sufficient land to feed them year round. Poverty, exacerbated by profligate taxes on Christian peasants, which continued even after the demise of the Ottoman Empire in the Balkans, was an important factor in Princip's decision to assassinate Ferdinand.[9] At the trial he stated that the people "are treated like cattle. The peasant is impoverished. They destroy him completely. I am a villager's son and I know how it is in the villages. Therefore I wanted to take my revenge, and I am not sorry."[10]

And yet Princip was an outsider among peasants, more the intellectual than the labourer. His school friend, Božidar Tomić, remembered him in his biography: "Even before he went to school, as he walked behind his calves, he liked to pretend that he was a schoolboy, carrying a bag on his back with some old books."[11] A small, bony kid with blue eyes, curly hair, and a pointed chin like his mother's, he preferred to be by himself and with his calves than with boys his age. As they played and the

other villagers toiled in the hot summer fields, he lost himself in daydreams. But the dreamer was no pushover. "When playing," Tomić recalled, "he was very rough, often striking boys stronger than he, especially if he felt that they were doing wrong to him or that the stronger ones were slighting him."[12] When Princip himself thought back to those days in an interview with the psychiatrist Martin Pappenheim in Theresienstadt—which the latter recorded in stenographic notes—he chose not to remember the fights but instead the solitary hours with books. "Was not much with other schoolboys, always alone. Was always quiet, sentimental child. Always earnest, with books, pictures, etc."[13] For the peasants who knew him, excessive learning explained his diminutive size and need to be alone. "See what a book can do to a human being," was the likely refrain. "To hell with books, use your brains."

His father agreed. He didn't let his son attend school until his ninth year, when his mother intervened. Besides exhibiting the peasant's traditional prejudice against formal learning, Petar Princip had practical reasons for keeping his son at home; he needed a shepherd to guard his sheep. But in the end he relented. Few parents today would disagree with his decision, but it turned out to be more pivotal than Petar Princip could have imagined. He didn't realize that educating the boy, which eventually meant sending him away, would expose him to radical ideas germinating among students at the time.

✦ We approached Gornji Obljaj, passing a little chapel by the road. It was evening, and the setting sun shone its golden light on the stone. Over the iron gates of the cemetery, far in the distance, I could see the mountain I'd noticed on the way in—serene, unchanging.

< *Gavrilo Princip's parents in Gornji Obljaj.* [from Dedijer, Sarajevo 1914, p. 944]

Near the hamlet, a brown horse wheeled powerfully on its tether, and the dirt road narrowed into an alley between very old, mostly destroyed stone houses. These were almost all roofless and long uninhabited. Other houses in the hamlet were made of brick and looked as though they'd been built during the last thirty years. The smell of urine welcomed us when we stepped out of the car. As we walked around, we saw an old woman peering tooth-lessly out at us from a broken window. A boy passed by on a bike, a soccer ball clamped on his rack. In a few years, I thought, he would realize there wasn't anything for him in Gornji Obljaj, if he didn't know it already, and he would leave for a life somewhere else. In this sense, not much had changed since Princip's day. The hamlet was still a sad, lifeless place the world had forgotten. And yet, when I looked between the broken houses at the valley in the distance, where a few gardens grew in square patches here and there, where someone walked on a dirt path that dawdled toward another hamlet, and as the fresh air of the silent evening settled around me, I found the place attractive in a peaceful way. I saw its beauty and I understood how one could be loyal to it.

The first person we spoke to in Gornji Obljaj, a tall man around seventy-five years of age with dark, droopy eyes and a UN ball cap aslant his head, turned out to be Mihajlo Princip, the very last Princip in the entire area, he told us, though he didn't say what the relationship was.

"This," he said with a dignified wave of his hand, "was Gavrilo Princip's house." We were looking at a gutted roofless structure, made of clean-cut, white stone blocks with a low door and two windows. Obviously, there was no museum anymore. A pang of disappointment shot through me. I went through the low door and walked inside the walls. There were a few burned ceramic pots, possibly signs of the Croats' attack in the last war, but noth-ing with the look of an authentic relic. As I looked around, I

> Top: Chapel by the road near Gornji Obljaj. Bottom: The hamlet of Gornji Obljaj.

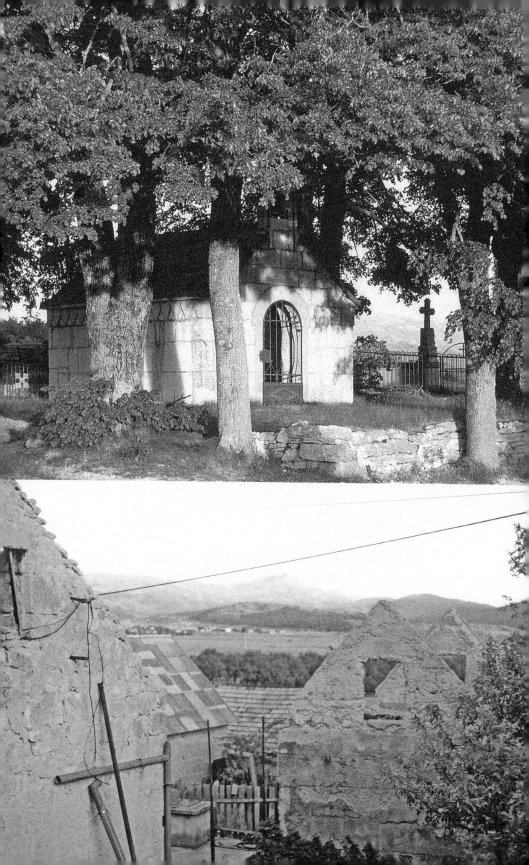

The remnants of the house where Gavrilo Princip was born.

struggled to feel a trace of Princip's presence. There was something wrong, I thought, about the evenness of the stone blocks, which made me suspect that the gutted house next door, a much older building to my eye, was a better candidate for Princip's house.

I based this conclusion on what I'd read about the original structure, which was apparently centuries old even by the time Princip was born, and which was described as "Bosnian Gothic."

In the old house the doors are small, and so very low that you can enter the house only by bowing your head. Inside it is dark. The house has no windows; instead of floor only beaten earth. To the left from the door is a stone bench on which a wooden barrel for water was standing; behind this, on a shelf, some cooking utensils, earthenware pots; a big round low table was hanging against the wall. On the other side of the door were three wooden

chests, a box for keeping flour, a sieve and another shelf. Deep on the right
side there was a low door leading to a small room in which stood a bed. On
the left side of the main part of the house was an open hearth, burning day
and night, surrounded by a low stone wall. Above it stood a verige, an iron
chain descending from the ceiling, on which were metal cauldrons hooked
above the fire. Smoke went through a badza, a hole in the roof above the
open fireplace. The only light in the house came through it.[14]

Princip's own eery memories of the home suggest he had few
regrets about leaving it. "The wet logs on the open fire gave the
only light to the closely packed *kmets* and their wives, wrapped
in thick smoke. If I tried to penetrate the curtain of smoke, the
most that I could see were the eyes of human beings, numerous, sad and glaring with some kind of fluid light coming from
nowhere. Some kind of reproach, even threat, radiated from
them, and many times since then they have awakened me from
my dreams."[15] The hamlet of Gornji Obljaj, with its narrow alleys
and old stone buildings, gave me a sense of this peasant world,
but the house itself was less evocative. For me it was a marker of a
more recent past.

"This house was burned in the last war," said Mihajlo, "just
like my own place. I barely made it to Banja Luka. My horse saved
my skin."

Of his three sons, only one had visited Gornji Obljaj since 1995.
The other two were on the move, with no fixed address, somewhere in Serbia. For anyone familiar with the former Yugoslavia,
their uncertain whereabouts suggest they were wanted here,
or would be targets for local Croats. Of course, their not coming back might also have been due to economics; a place with no
future isn't worth returning to, no matter whether it's Serbian or
Croatian—even if a father lives there.

Although Mihajlo generously offered us a glass of *travarica* (herb
brandy) on the concrete deck of his partially reconstructed house,
and while he said the war was a disaster ordinary people didn't

want, he seemed reluctant to divulge his real thoughts, especially about the Croats. They were, after all, the ones who had forced him to flee. Recognizing our Croatian ethnicity from our name and our accents, he held back out of politeness. We were all "ordinary people" so why risk the amicability of our brief relationship?

✦ After saying goodbye, we took a room in a destroyed town nearby called Bosansko Grahovo. The only hotel was owned by a Croat and looked to be intact, though the surrounding apartments, where the Serbs used to live, were mostly in ruins.

The hotel clerk, a tall, pinched, bleach-blonde wearing a push-up bra and a vacuous expression looked uncertainly at the distant mountain when I asked her its name. We were making small talk after negotiating the bill. As dusk was settling on the big valley, the evening sun spilled over the orange roofs of Gornji Obljaj a kilometre to the east and lit the face of the peak farther on.

"I was born in a village up the road," she shrugged, "so I don't know much about this area."

"I'll ask around," I answered.

"Yes, someone will know."[16]

I thought I'd make it easy for her, so I asked for the keys to the room. Her bovine eyes looked at me in confusion.

"No one has asked for keys before," she claimed, "but I'll see what I can do."

Later that evening, after returning from a drive through Bosansko Grahovo, we found a ring of black iron keys on the windowsill at the end of the hall. I tried them all but none fit the lock. Maybe the keys opened the other rooms, but I didn't have the patience to bother. I gave up and left the keys on the sill.

"What are you so worried about?" my father asked.

"I want to make sure no one comes in," I answered.

"No one is going to come in."

"How are you so sure? We're the only ones here; our car's the only one in the parking lot. Every normal place has keys to the doors."

"Listen, they've never used keys here. It's a small town, a safe place."

I wasn't so sure, but I had no choice except to get ready for the night. I took a shower in the communal washroom down the hall. Afterwards, in the room again, I pushed a chair against the door and settled into bed.

At first I was able to sleep, despite the savage baying of a dog somewhere outside my window. But in the middle of the night I woke up. I was back in Grahovo Polje in front of the old ruin where Princip was born. According to Božidar Tomić, Princip's house had no windows at all. The only source of light besides the door came from a gap in the ceiling where smoke from the open fire escaped. The house I saw with its two windows couldn't have been Princip's. I lay in the dark, disappointed, convinced that the building I'd seen was just an old man's invention.

Maybe it was possible, I thought after a while, for Mihajlo Princip both to believe his words and be absolutely wrong at the same time. If one can encapsulate Bosnians' interpretations of their own history, it might lie exactly in this combination of perfect self-assurance and complete error. Later, when I returned to Zagreb, I came across a book that explained the mystery of the Princip home. The stone shell I saw beside Mihajlo Princip's house is likely the remnant of a reconstructed building, a museum, which was built upon the original, also destroyed by the Croats, but this time during the Second World War. It was ideologically significant that in the Muslim–Croatian sector of Bosnia, where Gornji Obljaj is located, no one with the money or authority had the interest to reconstruct Princip's birthplace.

2 ✦ THE KRAJINA, TRAVNIK, SARAJEVO

✦ FROM COUNTRY TO CITY

THE NEXT MORNING dawned bright and sunny. The big dog that had barked ferociously during the night had finally gone to sleep, and the owner of the hotel was watering his flowers. His care for his rundown place seemed hopeless and touching at the same time. He told us he'd been trying to repair the hotel ever since the war but was having trouble finding workers.

"Young people here don't want a job. I hired one guy to move some logs, and he was at it for a few minutes, then he quit. Said it was too hard and went home. Just like that. Another kid was supposed to cut branches from that tree—see over there, I wanted guests to have a nice view of the valley—but he took one look and told me it was too dangerous! Said he didn't want to fall and hurt himself!" The hotel owner turned his thick bald head back to us and laughed. "Life is easy when grandma gets a pension, so why work?"

My father had found another point of contact with a Bosnian. He, too, knew the dilemma of finding reliable workers, in his case for his stonework business in Vancouver. I saw him nodding understandingly as the man spoke. So I was surprised when he told me later that he thought the guy wasn't telling us the whole story.

"How do you mean?" I asked.

"Maybe he couldn't get workers because he was Croatian and they were Serbs. Maybe people thought they were doing *him* a favour."

"Could be," I answered.

"Maybe they resented him having more than they did."

"But he told us there were no problems at all between people here," I said.

"There are always problems."

"Well, you yourself said this was a friendly, safe place."

"Friendly to outsiders. Not friendly to each other." He gave me a wry smile that usually went along with that cackle of his. "This is Bosnia, sonny boy, not Newfieland."

We were driving southeast toward Sarajevo on a road that bisected another long valley called Livanjsko Polje, which paralleled the Dinaric range and the Croatian border to our right. The new blacktop meandered pleasantly past fallow fields, a few vegetable gardens, and occasionally the broken shells of houses. Now and again we saw a farmer at work in his field. Never a well-populated valley, it seemed lonelier than ever.

I stopped when I saw a man sitting on the porch of his shack and a cow grazing at the edge of the road. The cow's hip bones stuck out grotesquely like those of drought-stricken beasts in Africa. Its owner got off his chair and hobbled down the steps when we approached. He was fat, narrow-eyed, and unshaven, the thick bristles of his beard like black wires. As we spoke he did

> Ivan Dulundijak in a cemetery near Livno.

a two-step, treading from one foot to another. He grunted curt answers in a low monotonous voice, telling us he'd grown up in Bosansko Grahovo, had never married, and had stayed here during the war. He owned a bit of land and some animals but survived mainly on his pension. To me it seemed as if life had taken its toll on him, but his spirit wasn't all gone, as I found out. When my father mentioned we'd spent the night in Bosansko Grahovo, in the hotel belonging to the Croat, his two-step stopped and his dull eyes swung at him with the weight of an axe.

We returned to our car and drove on. Livanjsko Polje was bordered to the south by the Dinaric massif and to the north by the Staretina mountains. This valley was more given over to agriculture than Princip's Grahovo Polje, the soil marshy in places and showing signs of the alluvial richness Vladimir Dedijer claimed was characteristic of the area around Gornji Obljaj. We had entered a Croat-populated region.

The first Croat we met was clearing his family's plot in a roadside cemetery. Around the Catholic chapel were impressive granite headstones like the ones we'd seen in Lipo, but here there were few rickety wood or iron crosses. Green geckos sunned themselves on the stones. A short man with grey hair plastered across his sweaty forehead, he slid his sharpening stone into a tin cup on his hip, leaned on his scythe and told us about his life here. Ivan Dulunđijak described his trips on foot across the Dinara Mountains to the Dalmatian Coast in the 1950s, where he sought work cutting hay. He wore out his shoes during those travels, spent many nights out in the open, and worked long hours in the blistering heat. But despite the hard work he looked back fondly on those times.

"I was young and healthy. Nothing bothered me too much. And the Dalmatian girls!" he smiled roguishly, "I wasn't a married man yet..."

Ivan's travels reminded me of the long peripatetic tradition in Bosnia-Herzegovina. Princip's generation hiked great distances mainly in search of work and education. Many travelled to Serbia to join the irregular forces in the Turkish Wars. Unlike Ivan's trips in the 1950s, the travels of Princip's generation took their toll physically; long days, missed meals, nights outdoors in variable weather, and the close quarters of flophouses cost many their health. Princip himself may have contracted tuberculosis before his imprisonment in Bohemia's Theresienstadt, where he died of the disease in 1918. But these journeys allowed Princip and other young men to experience firsthand the difficult, restricted lives most Bosnians could expect to lead under Austro-Hungarian rule. The travels of Ivan and others of his generation had no such political undertones.

As we spoke I got the impression that Ivan's life hadn't been full of adventures, save for those early ones. He'd grown up in the village near the cemetery, a scattering of orange-tiled houses built against the hills, and he had lived most of his life in the small city of Livno. Now, the village was mainly deserted, many of the houses destroyed. His aging mother was one of the few who refused to leave, still living in the house where he was born.

The fighting that did the damage took place in 1995, when Croatian units of the Bosnian army and the Croatian army drove out the militant Serbs. "They started this business, so they had it coming," he said, not concealing his satisfaction. My father asked him why some homes were hit, while others were spared, and he said that it was due to chance.

"What will happen if the Serbs return?" I asked.

"If the good ones come back, no problem. Otherwise forget it. The most important thing is for them not to hate us."

In the car later my father told me he doubted Ivan's explanation about which houses had been hit and which spared. "Maybe he's right about this village. But I can tell you, there were plenty of houses that were hit on purpose in Bosnia. A Serb commander knew which house in the village belonged to a Muslim, and he wanted to get revenge for something. So he ordered it destroyed."

✦ At Livno we turned north toward central Bosnia-Herzegovina. This was the same route young Princip followed on the way to the Habsburg Military School in Sarajevo. It took three days on horseback for him and his father to arrive in Bugojno, from where they took the train the rest of the way. The journey was a momentous one for the boy, and not just because he was leaving home for the first time. Long distances by horse, unfamiliar terrain, the strange atmosphere of Muslim villages all disturbed and frightened him. At one point he ran from the Muslim *han* where his father intended to spend the night, crying, "I don't want to sleep there. They're Turks."[1]

At first glance the rugged, karst-limestone terrain leading to Bugojno resembles that of the Dalmatian coast but without the sea to relieve the land's emptiness and austerity. Here there is only open sky and long vistas across big plateaux and occasionally pastures of wild grass thinly carpeting the white rocks. I saw another underfed cow chained to a stick, grazing among the stones on a vast field. A widow wearing black yelled a cheery hello from her house on the other side of the highway when I stopped to take a photo. So solitary was her life in this empty place that she seemed eager to talk to any stranger. My father and I continued on, past some signs for skiing, an alpine lodge, and a few narrow gravel roads that headed up into the karst mountains in perfectly straight lines, as though they were in a hurry to get somewhere. Soon we entered the hilly, wooded country around Bugojno. As we approached Travnik, we saw Muslim cemeteries with their thin, white headstones perched on tiny, steeply slanted patches of land beside the road. Slim haystacks poked out of small fields, and the minarets of mosques rose above each village. Outside garishly coloured roadhouses—bright yellow and blue—sheep roasted on spits atop giant barbecues.

Travnik was once the seat of the Ottoman viziers in Bosnia-Herzegovina. Located below a medieval fortress at the foot of Mount Vlašić, one of the country's highest peaks (1,943 metres), the city used to be an important trading place for travellers and peddlers from Serbia, Ragusa (as Dubrovnik was formerly known), and other parts of the Ottoman Balkans. Although much of the city was destroyed by fire in 1903, you can still see mosques from the Ottoman period, a Turkish museum, a covered market, and the home of Bosnian Nobel Laureate Ivo Andrić, author of *Travnik Chronicles* and other historical novels.

On the main drag, a few stores sold Bosnian carpets, red and black and white in various geometrical designs; silver and copper serving plates; and copper coffee pots engraved with the word "Sarajevo." A graveyard beside a mosque had some old headstones. One was a narrow, grey slab at the foot of a crumbling, weedy sarcophagus with a triangular top and twin bas-reliefs of cypresses. The mosque was a square, nondescript building, save for its pretty doors, which were embossed with shapes like the turbans on male headstones and painted green, turquoise, and orange, under an arch of the same colours.

Three old men wearing black berets were chatting outside. Politely I asked them if they'd be willing to pose for a picture. Without answering, they got up as one and went into the mosque, closing the door behind them. A few seconds later, a squat elderly man came out, wearing black leather slippers and a pale blue, short-sleeved shirt unbuttoned to his chest. This, evidently, was the *hoḍa*. When I told him I'd asked the others for a photo, he said, "Would you like one of me?"

While I was speaking I had approached the mosque's entrance, and he quickly shut the door behind himself. "Sure," I said, stepping back, "that would be fine."

Without another word, he sat down on a bench outside the mosque, collected himself, and stretched both arms out with his palms facing up. He stayed in this position, with his eyes closed, for about ten seconds. He held his hands over his face for about the same length of time then gazed thoughtfully into empty space. And that was that. I had just enough time to focus my

camera and snap a few pictures before he got up abruptly, looked once in my direction and returned to the mosque without a word.

In the car again, I told my father about the *hoða*'s behaviour. "The guy's a bigshot here" my father replied. "And you're a nobody."

"That's about it," I said.

"But you know," he went on, "he's a dignified man, a serious man. Maybe he didn't like the feeling of being photographed. He felt like an animal in a zoo."

"He could have stayed to talk."

"Look, he's got things to do. He's busy. And you're just a tourist."

"A nobody."

"That's right," he laughed.

✦ After Travnik, the highway took us on to Sarajevo, past ugly factories overgrown with trees and on past small, orange-tiled houses, gardens, and sheep pastures of a pre-industrial world. These villages seemed to belong to the hilly Bosnian landscape and I thought that they would be similar to what Princip saw as he passed through in 1909.

Soon we entered a newly rebuilt outer sector of postwar Sarajevo. Amazingly, it looked untouched. Not a single bullet hole was to be seen on the bright, glittering shopping centres, the new businesses, the banks and car dealerships that lined the main drags. Cars ripped past us hell bent for somewhere, their drivers angrily honking at us to get moving or get out of the way.

Suddenly, with the narrowing of the street, I realized we'd come to the Appel Quay, as the long avenue beside the Miljacka River was called in Princip's day, where the conspirators waited for the archduke's arrival. On the left we saw a long row of sooty, Austrian-era buildings, to the right the high hills that gave

< *The hoða in Travnik.*

Serbian units virtually unassailable positions from which to bomb the city between 1992 and 1995. Sarajevans used to ascend Mount Trebević by cable car and picnic on the verdant slopes, but the Serbs littered it with mines, and now it is called the "lost mountain." I tried to imagine the hills around Sarajevo as they must have looked in 1914. Mentally, I erased most of the houses that clung to the steep slopes, as well as the new, white grave markers of a sprawling Muslim cemetery, and I was there.

In 1911, Princip and some high-school friends climbed to the tourist hut on nearby Mount Bjelašnica, where he allegedly wrote an inscription in the souvenir book. His joy at the summer holidays stretching in front of him, his heightened sensitivity to nature, and his romantic longings hinted at toward the end of the passage reveal a different Princip than the hardened, radical one of history:

Gone are the days of annoyance and boredom behind the dirty scribbled desks—holidays are here. After three days of celebration at home, we decided to enliven these hot and boring days—and travel somewhere—let us go to the Bjelašnica Mountain and beyond; no sooner said than done. We left Hadžići at sunset when the western sun was blazing in purple splendor, when the numberless rays of the blood-red sun filled the whole sky and when the whole of nature was preparing to sleep through the beautiful, dreamy summer evening in the magic peace—that beloved, ideal night of the poet. Walking briskly, we reached the foot of Bjelašnica Mountain, boasting of our speed and wiping large beads of sweat from our brows. After a short rest and a bite at the edge of the forest, we started to climb....

Without a word we progressed hesitantly through the forest, entranced by the magic, deep silence, listening to the whisperings of the sweet-smelling flowers and motionless trees. Following our noses, we struggled upward through the thick forest; we looked at each other despairingly when we were surrounded by hellish darkness, which seemed like the laughter of ugly monsters. A light, faint shudder went through our rather weary limbs, and we continued to march upward in silence, lumbering over fallen trunks and

scattered branches. Heavens, how many times the thought went through
my mind that I would be hurled into some bottomless precipice.

We could go no further. We ate our frugal supper. We built a fire—the
best sight I ever saw. No poet has ever described it better....

My companions fell asleep around the fire. I could not. I was sleepy, I
dozed, but how could one sleep in this empire of brooding illusions....

My companions burrowed into the leaves, and I sang, dreamed and
prayed to my secret; oh, what sweet and painful moments in the beautiful
time before the dawn, sweeter than sleep....[2]

We parked in the old town and walked along the very streets
where the assassins once did. I saw them in their black suits and
ties passing among the living. They flitted among groups of young
nubile women, whose scanty attire Princip would have disap-
proved of; they passed through the warren of tight, cobbled lanes
of Baščaršija, the Turkish Quarter, where tinkers still hammered
out copper coffee pots and low-roofed shops still sold them, and
they wandered into the Austrian section, whose tall, rigid, rectangular buildings appeared suddenly on the main boulevard like a
border of a new country. Around me persisted the signs of 1914 in
the form of an old man's felt fedora or a stifling, smoky café where
men drank Turkish coffee, downed shots of *rakija*, gossiped, and
talked politics. For me, the Sarajevo of 1914 merged with the present one, and every living person on the old, unchanging streets
seemed unsubstantial, impermanent, like white smudges in a
daguerreotype.

We continued to walk through the old city, stopping for a
moment in front of the Begova Džamija, or Beg's Mosque, which
was built in 1531. In the shade of its veranda, women sat chatting on one end, men on the other. The former relaxed against the
mosque, shoes discarded, their heads covered in bright scarves.
Vaguely Middle Eastern in appearance, the women seemed used
to people taking pictures of them and looked pleased by the attention. To the right, the men walked up and down the steps of the

Tourist shop in the Baščaršija Quarter of Sarajevo. Right: Austrian-era buildings in Sarajevo.

veranda to the fountain in the courtyard, where they washed their hands, faces, and feet, and then put on slippers before entering the mosque. When they were finished, they left the slippers in a row on the veranda. As everything went on calmly, uninterrupted by the world around, the thought came to me that the people here seemed so peaceful in these moments precisely because their rituals and their places in them were determined and held no surprises. Maybe there was a lesson here. In any case, I was impelled to stay a while in the quiet courtyard, listening to the birds, sheltered from the steady hum of the big city.

✦ Later that day, we made our way to Oprkanj Street, a narrow alley where the house belonging to Danilo Ilić's mother stood. I'd learned of its location from the Muslim guide at a nearby museum

dedicated to the period of the Austrian Occupation. The Sarajevans we'd spoken to had no idea of the house's whereabouts, nor any clue about Danilo Ilić. Yet they should have, because of the momentous part he played in their history.

It began in 1907, when Princip first arrived in Sarajevo to continue his schooling. Initially he was to enrol in the Habsburg Military School and become an officer in the empire. At the last moment, however, Princip's brother, Jovo, who'd been given responsibility for situating the boy after Petar Princip had dropped him off and returned home, was swayed by an acquaintance and decided to register the boy in the Merchants School instead. The man, a clothing store owner, convinced Jovo that his brother shouldn't become an executioner of his own people. And so Jovo found him a room in the house of a respectable widow, Stoja Ilić, unaware that her son, Danilo, was a revolutionary in the making. His collection of books and ideas influenced Princip in his first years away from home. In 1907, Princip was just thirteen and Danilo seventeen, an age difference that determined the nature of their relationship—Ilić the mentor and master, Princip the innocent peasant from the country.

The son of a cobbler who died when he was only five years old, Danilo Ilić was born in 1891. A good student, he graduated from the Merchants School in 1905 and, with the aid of an Austrian government scholarship, finished Teachers College in 1912. He belonged to a new class of Serbian intellectuals born to peasants, teachers, journeymen, and Greek Orthodox village priests. These young men tended to be poor and unemployed because of the traditional preference in bureaucratic circles for Croats over Serbs. And so they were often radical in their views, "partly because they had no vested interest in the *status quo* and partly because they knew at firsthand the plight of the mass of the people."[3] Four years older than other graduates of the Teachers College, Ilić had spent

Danilo Ilić.
[from Dedijer, Sarajevo 1914, p. 981]

Right: Stoja Ilić's house in Sarajevo.

the years between 1905 and 1908 working as a newsboy and as an usher, prompter, and copyist in a travelling theatre (from which he was kicked out for some reason). After that, he began wandering on foot throughout Bosnia-Herzegovina, working variously as a labourer, railway porter, apprentice in a quarry, and longshoreman on the river Sava.

Ilić, though, was an intellectual, not a labourer. He proofread and wrote for various Sarajevo newspapers, and he translated works by Maxim Gorky, Oscar Wilde, Mikhail Bakunin, and others into Serbo-Croatian. He went on to teach in Avtovac (Herzegovina) and Foča (Bosnia) after graduating from Teachers College in 1912, while six out of the nine members of his class volunteered for guerrilla units in Serbia during the first Balkan War. Suffering from a stomach ulcer, however, he went back to Sarajevo, where he worked as a clerk in the Serbian National Bank until June 1913. Ilić's decision was pragmatic, but it also indicated his distaste for

(and possibly fear of) armed conflict. Instead of volunteering for the front lines, he served as a nurse in the cholera wards of the Serbian army in 1913. He was hospitalized for a month and a half after the Balkan Wars, possibly from another stomach ulcer.

The house where Ilić and Princip roomed looked very much like it did in a photo from the 1930s. It was a pale ochre two-storey with large windows on the second floor and a walled-in garden. Lacking the bearing of a significant building, it had just become another house in a crammed section of town. I wondered if the present owners had any inkling about the former tenants. The man who answered the door had about as much desire to talk to me as a kid looks forward to a needle. His stern face didn't react when I explained my purpose in coming to Sarajevo and when I asked him about Gavrilo Princip.

"Of course we've always known about the house," he finally said, continuing to hold the door slightly ajar, his head poking out warily. "But who cares what happened a hundred years ago? It's not something that concerns us. Plus, there's too much history in this country anyway." And with that he politely excused himself and shut the door.

✦ I continued my walk through Sarajevo's old quarter, unable to rid myself of the assassins' haunting presence on the streets. I thought of young Princip who spent much of his time in this neighbourhood, leaving when money was short to stay with his brother in nearby Ilidže. He was a good student, who focused on his studies and kept to himself. As he told Martin Pappenheim years later in Thersienstadt, he was always "solitary, always in libraries."[4] Contemporaries of his confirmed his interest in books; a former acquaintance of Princip's in Belgrade, Dobrosav Jevdjević, offered a backhanded compliment in a letter read at the trial of the assassins, saying that "Gavrilo Princip stood out among them. He pretended that no one was better than he, especially in his knowledge of literature."[5] Like many young Bosnians, Princip wanted to be a poet. On one occasion, he nervously asked Bosnia's future Nobel laureate, Ivo Andrić, to look over a poem he had written. When he didn't bring it, Andrić asked him why and Princip answered casually that he had destroyed it.[6]

Besides literature, many young men of Princip's generation had political interests. *Mlada Bosna* or "Young Bosnia" is the title for the amorphous grouping of secret societies that sought to end Austro-Hungarian occupation, though no formal organization of that name existed at the time. The majority appeared to have been Serbs, but Croats and Muslims also filled their ranks. Even though the ultimate goal of these societies was the destruction of the Habsburg Empire, and its replacement with some form of South Slavic union, they weren't only nationalistic in orientation. The hard core of Young Bosnians also wanted to overcome Bosnia's primitivism, which included its feudalistic agrarian condition. As Dedijer notes, they "challenged the existing institutions of state, school, church and family, and they believed in egalitarianism and the emancipation of women. For that reason ethics became a field of special interest for them."[7] Among the more reviled aspects of Austrian occupation for many Young Bosnians was the establishment of military brothels.

The liberalism of *Mlada Bosna* was tempered by an ascetic streak that for me seems linked in spirit with the practices and beliefs of the ancient Bosnian Bogomils.[8] This asceticism was due partly to poverty and partly to the intense, radical commitment demanded by revolutionary activity. Many Young Bosnians renounced family ties and abstained from liquor and sex. This repudiation of worldly contacts and pleasures wasn't universal among all the conspirators in 1914 (many of the older men charged in the conspiracy to kill Ferdinand were married and enjoyed their *šljivovica*), but it is true of the young insurgents living in Austrian-occupied Bosnia, Princip among them. It is also possible that in Princip's case his father's conservatism rubbed off on him. In general, the Young Bosnians distinguished themselves from older, more conservative revolutionaries, such as Vladimir Gaćinović, who was influenced by theories on gradual social revolution.

The political situation at the time undoubtedly hurried this departure from gradualism. Besides the annexation of Bosnia by the Habsburgs in 1908, other events swept many young men away on waves of social unrest. A rash of assassination attempts followed in the wake of the Zagreb Treason Trials (trumped-up charges against fifty-three Serbs of conspiring to unite Croatia and Bosnia-Herzegovina with Serbia). Bosnian Croat Luka Jukić attempted to shoot the *ban* of Croatia, Count Slavko Cuvaj, on June 8, 1912, in Zagreb, but wounded three and killed one police-man instead. Even though the assassination attempt took place in neighbouring Croatia, the unrest leading up to it spilled into Bosnia, and the plot itself included students from Croatia, Bosnia, and the secret societies in Serbia.[9] Young Croats who were dis-satisfied at the capitulation of the Croat-Serb coalition took to the streets and fought armed battles against police. Students in Slovenia, Croatia, Bosnia, and Herzegovina showed their support in further demonstrations. Luka Jukić and a Dalmatian student, Oskar Tartalja, visited Sarajevo in February to organize rallies against the Habsburgs. According to one student's diary, Princip went from class to class, "threatening with his knuckle-duster all the boys who wavered in coming to the new demonstrations."[10]

Other assassination attempts were to come,[11] but the most con-sequential for Princip and his fellow assassins was the attempt made in 1912 by a depressive Bosnian-Serb law student, Bogdan Žerajić, against then governor of Bosnia, Marijan Varešanin. Having failed to assassinate Emperor Franz Josef in 1910 (appar-ently out of pity for the emperor's age), Žerajić blasted five shots at the governor by the Lateiner Bridge in Sarajevo, missed with every one of them, and saved the last for himself. In the legend that grew around Žerajić, the governor kicked the dead body and castigated it with the epithet "you scum." Whatever the specif-ics, the example of Žerajić to the (mainly Serbian) youth of Bosnia was monumental, despite his failure. Bosnian-Serb revolutionary Vladimir Gaćinović wrote an influential pamphlet on Žerajić called "The Death of a Hero." After moments of "great national failure," Gaćinović said, referring to the annexation, "there comes upon the stage a man of action, of strength, of life and virtue, a type such as opens an epoch, proclaims ideas, and enlivens suffering and spellbound hearts." He quoted Žerajić's last words, "I leave it to Serbdom to avenge me," and then asked, "Young Serbs, will you produce such men?"[12]

For non-Serbs, the reverence for Bogdan Žerajić's pathological self-sacrifice seems incredible, but his actions had a desperate logic in the minds of Bosnian-Serb youth. When Princip returned from Belgrade before the assassination, he apparently carried a handful of Serbian soil and sprinkled it on Žerajić's unmarked grave in the section of the cemetery reserved for suicides. On the eve of the assassination he went to the grave again for a final communion.

This was a critical time in Princip's life. Besides his involvement in student demonstrations, for which he was expelled from school, he made the momentous decision in the spring of 1912 to walk to Belgrade.[13] In the interview with Martin Pappenheim, Princip said he told "nobody about it. Father and brother would not send any money. Promised to be a good student. Then they agreed with his remaining in Belgrade."[14] His decision was also partly motivated by the loss of his stipend from the Serbian welfare society Prosvjeta after having been sick and failing a class in mathematics (his first failure). The move to Belgrade led him further than ever from his family, geographically and spiritually.

Had he never gone to Belgrade, another life might have awaited him in Sarajevo. He fell in love in 1911. Although he refused to identify the girl when he spoke to Pappenheim, only mentioning that the relationship was platonic ("ideal love, never kissed"[15]) and that he had never written her, he might have also had feelings for Vukosava Čabrinović, the younger sister of Princip's co-conspirator

42 BOSNIA

Nedeljko. When she was twelve, fifteen-year-old Princip found her reading a dime novel called *The Secrets of the Istanbul Palace*, and instead introduced her to the stories of Oscar Wilde and a novel by a young Serb writer named Milutin Uskoković. A correspondence followed in which Princip sent her books, copies of famous paintings, and poems he had written. In thanks for his attempt to educate her and broaden her mind, she pawned her golden cross and sent money to Princip and her brother, who were struggling to survive in Belgrade in the winter of 1913–1914. After the assassination, she buried his letters and poems in Duži, Herzegovina, where they were lost forever. Therefore, no evidence of the correspondence exists except Dobrosav Jevdjević's reconstructions based on her memories. It was Jevdejević's letter that was read at the trial of the assassins in 1914. Princip, he noted gratuitously, "had a rather intimate correspondence" with Vukosava Čabrinović. "He told me what an upright girl she was."[16]

✦ Vukosava's brother, Nedeljko Čabrinović, was born in Sarajevo on January 20, 1895, the oldest of nine children. When Princip met him in 1912, Nedeljko was a handsome, lanky teenager, son of Vaso Čabrinović, the owner of a prosperous café in Sarajevo whose licence had been issued in exchange for his services as an informant for the Austro-Hungarian police. While the father's police activities caused friction between father and son, the root of their problems was the old man's parental methods. He meted out his iron-fisted rule with heavy beatings and verbal abuse. Even his wife and daughters weren't spared completely, if we are to judge by a sympathetic letter Nedeljko wrote to Vukosava while he was studying at the Merchants School in Trebinje. When his son transferred to Sarajevo during the 1907–1908 school year, and promptly failed the year, his father was furious, took him out of school, and apprenticed him to a locksmith. "That was in the eighth or ninth

< *Young Nedeljko Čabrinović, with parents and sister Vukosava.*
[*from Dedijer,* Sarajevo 1914, *p. 972*]

month of school," Nedeljko recalled at the trial. "I was sick. The curriculum was not the same and I failed in many subjects. My father was angry, hated me and mistreated me, and I ran away from home. I tried to learn a trade. I was all on my own."[17]

His father's knee-jerk decision to apprentice his son marked the end of Nedeljko's school education. Čabrinović gave up his first trade then quit his second apprenticeship—to a lathe operator—before he settled on typesetting. This seemed an appropriate choice, since it kept him in contact with the world of ideas. He continued to read regularly, mainly revolutionary writing, such as *The Communist Manifesto*, Chernishevsky's *What is to be Done?*, and William Morris's *News From Nowhere*. He put pen to paper, too; at fourteen, he wrote a speech when he was voted the first president of the Printers' Apprentice Guild, and he wrote an article in 1912 in the Sarajevo paper *Srpska Riječ* criticizing the Social Democratic leadership's undemocratic methods. The party's paper, *Glas Slobode*, sharply criticized his article, made allegations against him of espionage for the Serbian state, as well as insinuations about his father's police activities. At Princip's trial, an acquaintance of Čabrinović's said that this disagreement with the Socialist Party, which resulted in his being expelled, was the moment he "became a Serb."[18] Despite these intellectual efforts and political activities, his lack of a formal education was probably at the root of Princip's snobbish attitude toward Čabrinović.

Early in his work life Čabrinović proved adept at mouthing off. This was likely why an elderly locksmith branded him on the neck with a piece of red-hot iron, and another older worker at the Serbian printing plant in Sarajevo slapped him. In reaction to the first incident, thirteen-year-old Čabrinović ran away from home, and, as a result of the second, he quit his job of two years, was kicked out by his father, and went to Zagreb, where he tried to find work for a month but was forced to return. He left once more after his father had the police imprison him for three days when he refused to apologize to a servant girl after an argument; he walked all the way to Novi Sad, some 145 kilometres from Sarajevo, and worked there for a while before finding a job in a monastery printing plant in Karlovci, then in another printing plant in Šid run by the Social Democratic Party of Croatia.

His most important brush with authority (and the law) occurred in 1912, during a strike at a printing plant in Sarajevo. He was kicked out of the house again after refusing to obey his father's wish that he not participate; he went to live with the anarchist leader of the strikers, Stevan Obilić, travelled to Zenica north of Sarajevo to warn printers arriving by train not to break the strike, was arrested by police, who had been monitoring his actions, and was imprisoned for three days for planning to set fire to some printing shops, one of which was owned by Sarajevo's Catholic Archbishop Stadler. Čabrinović's refusal to reveal Obilić's name resulted in his banishment from Sarajevo for five years.

This was a decisive moment in Čabrinović's life. At the trial, he remembered the banishment bitterly:

> I was driven by personal motives of revenge. I began to deliberate about the assassination for the first time when I was driven from Sarajevo. I did not like it, that a foreigner who came into our land, could drive me from my home. When I was expelled I was ordered to go to the lieutenant-governor, Rohony. I thought that he would pardon me for the offense for which I had been convicted, but he didn't. Instead, his secretary read me a moral sermon on life from his point of view and gave orders to show me the door. I was sorry that I didn't have weapons then, I would have blasted him with all six shots.[19]

Although his father managed to have the banishment lifted, Nedeljko Čabrinović would never find peace in Sarajevo. The pattern of conflict at work or at home, sudden departure, then return, would repeat itself throughout his short life. It seemed destined to continue after father and son fought yet again just before the assassination, but for the last time as it turned out, since Čabrinović was never to return home.

Emotional, temperamental, and troubled, Nedeljko Čabrinović packed considerable restlessness and conflict into his few years. More than any of the other conspirators he had a reputation both among the Sarajevo police and the local political establishment. As time went on, he saw his rebellion against the Austro-Hungarian regime as an extension of his personal conflict with his father. The assassination he had begun planning became a kind of patricide.

This glance at Čabrinović's life could lead one inevitably to the conclusion arrived at by Edith Durham in *The Serajevo* [sic] *Crime*. "In his brief career Chabrinovitch was a bad son, a bad scholar and a bad workman, for on his own showing he never kept a job longer than a few months. He was ready to murder anyone who opposed what he called 'his ideals.'"[20] And yet her harsh and partly errone-ous characterization conveniently glossed over Vaso Čabrinović's role in shaping his son's life. As Nedeljko said at the trial: "the upbringing he gave me brought me to this."[21]

✦ On our second day in Sarajevo I struck up a conversation with a shop owner whose son had never returned home either. At first, Ahmed Čačić, a short man with a pointed face and a trimmed, white beard, told us his life in Sarajevo these days was "*odličan*" (beautiful). He said it loudly and with conviction. With too much conviction, I thought. Sure enough, after a few minutes he told us with equal assurance that there was "no way" he would ever have a friendship with another Serb again.

"Not today, not tomorrow, not ever!" He paused for a second. "And I'll tell you why," he went on. "The reason is that I lost my son in this war. A sniper killed him. He was too young to die, just nineteen." Ahmed got up and went to the open door. He stood there looking out into the street, his back to us. The thought came to me that this was Čabrinović's age in 1914. At nineteen he died, too, in a sense, condemned to a slow death in solitary confinement in Theresienstadt. I wondered if his father mourned his loss as deeply as Ahmed did his.

"Would you like a coffee?" Ahmed asked finally, turning around.

"That would be fine," my father said.

Ahmed waved over a kid who was passing by and slipped a bill into his hand. Later, as we stood at the counter drinking sweet, thick Turkish coffee from tiny white cups, his mood improved. He told us he was making a modest living now after rebuilding his shop, which had been hit during the war. Most of Sarajevo had been rebuilt, and life had regained a kind of normalcy, but the city would never be what it was, at least not in his lifetime. Like many people we would meet, he painted an idealistic picture of multicultural harmony in pre-war Sarajevo.

"No one can just forget what those maniacs in the hills did to us. It's impossible to have a normal conversation."

"But didn't some Serbs suffer in Sarajevo during the siege?"

"Probably there were some, but they never hated their brothers," he claimed. "They took the same view."

I wasn't so sure of this, but decided not to press the matter. I guided the conversation further into the past and asked him what he thought of the assassins in 1914.

"Princip was a terrorist, plain and simple! They got rid of the Austrians in the end, but it would have been better if the Austrians had stayed."

Ahmed was alluding to the Habsburgs' ambitious civic works regime, which was on the scale of Napoleon's efforts in his so-called Illyrian provinces (part of present-day Croatia). Railways and bridges were built; industries like mining, chemicals, timber, projects of reforestation and agricultural research were begun. As one contemporary writer gushed enthusiastically, "We in England can form no conception of the marvellous transformation effected

here by Austria in that short space of time, nor even faintly realise the almost magical rapidity with which the recently barbaric provinces of Herzegovina and Bosnia have been converted into growing centres of commerce and civilisation."[22] But these changes didn't improve the lives of ordinary people, especially those of peasants. Even though the Habsburgs made adjustments to the Muslim landholding system, they maintained the basic hierarchical structure, which punished Christians the most. Perhaps for that reason there was widespread disenchantment about the Austrian-Hungarian presence among Bosnian Serbs but support among Bosnian Muslims.

There were other reasons for Serbs to be dissatisfied. The Young Bosnians considered the Austrian contribution to education as moribund as their efforts on the land-reform front. To Pappenheim, Princip cited the lack of schools in Bosnia, ten times fewer than in Serbia. Princip's figures, however, may have been skewed by his political biases. Hamilton Fish Armstrong put the number of elementary schools in Bosnia at 400 in 1914, and 1,172 in Serbia.[23] In support of Armstrong's figures, Noel Malcolm says "no government which builds nearly 200 primary schools, three high schools, a technical school and a teacher-training college can be described as utterly negligent in its educational policy. Peasants who refused to use iron ploughs were unlikely to rush to send their children to acquire an education which they themselves had never received."[24]

If there was disenchantment among the Serbs during the Austrian occupation, there was disenchantment during the Ottoman period, as well. A glance at Sarajevo's old quarter, whose Orthodox, Catholic, and Muslim architecture seems to suggest a marked religious and ethnic tolerance, actually reveals signs of social tension. For example, in 1872, a dispute broke out between the Orthodox community and Muslim clerics during the construction of the new

< Minaret and steeple in Sarajevo.

Orthodox cathedral in Sarajevo. The clerics insisted that the church should not exceed the height of the minaret of Beg's Mosque. They also protested against the ringing of church bells, not allowed up to that time in Ottoman cities. The fanatical *imam* protested to the new governor, the pragmatic Albanian Mehmed Akif-paša. When the *imam* cited the Koran, the governor said: "Silence, you donkey! You're not going to teach me the Koran! So you can't bear the sound of bells, can you, you dog? And the rest of you, are you such block-heads that you can't see that this scoundrel would ring the bells himself, so long as he were paid fifty groschen a month to do it?"[25]

✦ After bidding Ahmed goodbye, we walked along the congested Ferhadija promenade and into the narrow alleys that lead off from it like ribs from a spine. The Morića Han, a seventeenth-century caravansary for merchants and travellers on the ancient trade route across the Balkans, now housed restaurants, cafés, and shops. An arched, stone entry led us into a cobbled courtyard. In one of the former stables surrounding the courtyard a shop sold oriental rugs that hung from the ceiling and were piled in high stacks. Another stable had been converted into a restaurant, and it was there that we had a meal. On the white plaster walls, between dark wooden beams, were golden inscriptions in Arabic (which the waiters couldn't decipher). The restaurant's owner, in an attempt to add historical flavour, or most likely in the religious enthusiasm that nationalist jingoism took among Bosnia's Muslims after the war, had had the inscriptions made on the wall. There was nothing new or trendy about the menu, however. Besides *ražnići* or *ćevapčići* (spiced sausages), which are a ubiquitous "fast food" throughout the former Yugoslavia, you could order various kinds of *bureki* (phyllo pastry pies filled with ground meat, cheese, spinach, potatoes, or onions), *begova čorba* (veal and vegetable soup), or more widely Balkan specialties like *sarma* (meat and rice rolled in cabbage or vine leaves). I ordered a kind of cordon-bleu called *Sarajevski Steak*, a *Wiener Schnitzel* with cheese inside the folds of meat, served with slices of pita bread.

As we ate, alone in the restaurant, the two waiters smoked and played cards, and more of the sinewy Bosnian music we'd heard earlier during our trip played softly on the radio. We said nothing to each other for a while. Our long hours on the road over the last few days seemed to have caught up with us. In that moment, after the meal, I could easily have settled down in some quiet corner for a few hours rest. This was the end of the first stage of my journey, and we were about to return to Zagreb, but already I had plans for a trip to Serbia later that summer, and a seat ready for my father next year when we would complete our journey through Bosnia. We had travelled through this part of the world before, and we would travel together in the future. It occurred to me then that more than nineteen years had passed since I was nineteen years old.

3 ✦ BELGRADE

✦ CAPITAL OF THE SOUTH SLAVS

THE SERBIAN BORDER GUARD at Mali Zvornik glanced perfunc-
torily at my passport, handed it back, and waved me through.
I was relieved to have gotten through without any trouble. I'd
imagined the worst, mainly because of my own past experiences
with Serbian border guards in the former Yugoslavia, as well as
my father's stories of harassment over the years. But in addition, I'd built up numerous impressions about Serbia that had
led me to believe I would have a target on my back because of my
Croatian name. These worries were heightened by having to travel
alone, since my father had returned to Canada to finish a con-
tract. Nevertheless, I got on with the business of my journey. I
was headed to Belgrade, capital of Serbia and the "Piedmont" of
the South Slavs in 1914, where droves of Bosnian-Serb refugees
came to live at the time of the Balkan Wars. It was in Belgrade

that the conspirators arrived at the decision to assassinate Franz Ferdinand.

At first the road paralleled the green Drina River, on whose banks fishermen waited patiently in lawn chairs for a catch. Eventually the road wound northeast through hilly terrain and past congested villages nestled in the low hills. Sheep grazed peacefully in small meadows, women hoed their gardens, and young boys played soccer on flat, dirt patches between knee-high wooden posts. I passed what appeared to be a sawmill and a dreary factory. As on the Bosnian side of the border, no minarets were visible above the houses and all the signs were in Cyrillic. I felt just as much a foreigner as I had when I first heard the call to prayer in Velika Kladuša.

Near Šabac I passed an old farmhouse that belonged to Princip's era. It had a stone foundation, whitewashed walls, egg-blue shutters, and orange roof tiles covered by moss. A rickety wooden fence that ran around the cropped lawn was held tightly together by saplings, and in back were some rectangular wooden structures arranged in a row. To one side of the house was a veranda covered in grapevines, and beyond the wooden barn was a fruit orchard.

A girl was sitting out front selling *šljivovica* and jars filled with a dark, golden liquid. A sign among the jars read "200 dinars" (around four dollars). When I got out of my car and approached her, I realized she was older than I'd thought, around twenty, with long, black hair and large eyes almost as dark. Her delicate hands and pale skin, shaded blue under the eyes, told me she wasn't a farmer. In English that was much better than my Serbo-Croatian, she said she was an art student in Belgrade and was visiting her grandparents in the home where she'd spent much of her childhood.

I asked her about the jars, and she said they were her grandfather's honey. The hives were in the yard, in those rectangular boxes I'd spotted. "Would you like to see?" she asked.

I said I would, so she led me into the yard. The hives were inside three homemade boxes, which had slits on the sides for the bees to enter and leave. A panel on the front could be pulled out in order to reach the honey. Behind the boxes was a dark grey hay stack, no higher than my waist, which turned out to be another, older hive.

"That one's been there for as long as I can remember," she told me. "I was terrified of it when I was young. I would run into the kitchen whenever my grandfather would take out the honey. But of course I loved the honey itself. It amazed me that something so wonderful could come out of a place that was so frightening."

She said this with a light, infectious laugh. I liked the fact that she was here, far from her life in Belgrade, and I understood her feelings for her childhood home and for the old people who made it special. She had an artist's temperament (was a painter) and couldn't care less about history or politics. Or any of the other things that had brought me to Serbia. Still, she was invaluable to me, providing me with a picture of a different Serbia than the one I was used to. "I know nothing about politics," she went on to say. "Less than nothing! All I know is that they ruined our country."

We went back to the table where she asked, "Do you have room for some Serbian honey when you return to Canada?" I hesitated for a second, looking a little regretfully at the brandy bottles. "I might," I answered.

She handed me a glass jar, about ¾ of a litre, but refused my money. We argued back and forth good-naturedly, until I left the money on the table and drove on.

✦ Alone again, my thoughts returned to the past as I approached Belgrade. The First Balkan War in 1912, which pitted Bulgaria, Serbia, Montenegro, and Greece against the Ottoman Empire, and the Second Balkan War of 1913, in which Bulgaria attacked its erstwhile Balkan allies over the loss of territory, resulted in victory for the Serbs and a nationalistic euphoria even among other South Slavs who looked to Serbia for leadership in the new vector of power resulting from the defeat of the Turks and the belligerent presence of the Austrians. The Bosnian diaspora, who lived in precarious indigence in Serbia, sleeping in dog kennels when there was nowhere else, were among the most radical revolutionaries. Far from home, their country occupied, they breathed in the heady revolutionary air of restaurants and coffee houses.[1] As one historian said, "Many an idle hour was spent in the *kahvehane*, and many a 'dangerous thought' germinated there"[2]

Belgrade at this time was a hive of activity. Leon Trotsky described the city as it looked in October 1912, shortly before the First Balkan War:

> Belgrade has grown and has become cleaner and more handsome. There are new houses and shops, and they have begun paving the main street with wood blocks. Now, however, the city has a special air about it—on the alert, like a military camp. Everyone and everything is subordinated to the demands of the mobilization. Motorcars and cabs drive about almost exclusively on official business. The streets are full of mobilized men and men about to be mobilized. The shops are empty: there are no customers, and the number of clerks has been reduced to a minimum. Industry is at a standstill, apart from the branch that serves the needs of mobilization and the coming war. There is no labour to be had. A sugar factory in Belgrade has had to recruit twenty workers from abroad in order not to have to cease production altogether, while another sugar factory, at Cuprija, has been given permission by the government to employ prisoners. In Prince Michael Street, the city's main artery, work on road improvements has been suspended. Tramlines have been taken up over a long stretch, there are holes dug in the roadway, wood blocks are lying about, getting soaked in the rain, and a vehicle approaching the Moskva Hotel, the best in Belgrade, sinks into a puddle up to the hub of its wheels....In a stationer's shop a huge, symbolic battle picture is displayed. Having thrown down a frontier fence of sharp-pointed palings, the Serbs, picturesque and elegant, are bursting in,

*mounted on powerful horses, to the realm of the Turk, crushing and smash-
ing everything in their way."*[3]

This was the nationalistic atmosphere awaiting Gavrilo Princip
when he first arrived. On crossing the border, he knelt down and
kissed the Serbian earth. Although he had come to continue his
studies, the liberating nationalistic air soon made him keen to
take a leave from school and take up arms against the Turks. But
Serbia didn't repay his loyalty. Like thousands of other anonymous
Bosnians, he was swallowed by the metropolis, barely surviving
at first, in his case because his brother had refused to send him
money (help eventually arrived after he promised to finish the
fifth year of high school—which he went on to fail in June). When
Princip decided to enlist with the Serbian *komite* (irregular forces),
he was rejected at their Bosnian headquarters because of his small
size, though at his trial he claimed he was initially accepted and
that he headed to the town of Prokuplje, north of the Turkish frontier, where Serbian forces were massing.[4] After he "trained for
some time under arms," Major Vojislav Tankosić, leader of the
komite and a member of the Black Hand's Central Committee, took
one look at Princip then dismissed him with a wave of his hand:
"You are too small and too weak."[5] At his trial, Princip tried to
blame this humiliating rejection on an illness, but his shame
likely followed him to his brother's home in Hadžići where he
heard news of Serbia's successes on the front.

Just as Princip went through a turbulent time in Belgrade,
so, too, did Nedeljko Čabrinović. During his first stay, when he
worked at a printing plant that published the anarchist newspaper *Komuna* (The Commune), he became sick (possibly an early bout
with tuberculosis) and had to return home. Based on his account
at the trial, he received works by the anarchist Krsta Cicvarić and
took them home with him, only to have his mother burn most of
them.[6] After recovering from his illness for two months, becoming mixed up in the printers' strike of 1912, and being exiled for

five years, he returned to Belgrade. He managed to survive on occasional day jobs until he got word from his father that he had convinced authorities to have the sentence revoked. Wanting to go back, maybe partly because he thought things had improved between his father and himself, he went to the Serbian nationalist organization *Narodna Odbrana*[7] in the hopes of securing money for the trip. The major, Milan Vasić, noticed a book by Guy de Maupassant in Čabrinović's pocket. "He took it out of my pocket and asked, 'What is it?' When he saw the title, he said such reading was not for me and gave me a copy of *Narodna odbrana*...(Statutes of the *Narodna odbrana* and Popular Heroic Songs). Beside those books I received money [15 dinars]. 'I don't know how to thank you for your kindness,' I said to him, and he told me always to remain a good Serb."[8] With the money from Vasić, twenty crowns from the printer's union, in addition to an unexpected gift of travel money from his father, he bought books by the "best known socialist writers: Zola, Tolstoy, Krapotkin," put them in a suitcase, and mailed it to Sarajevo. Instead of spending the money his father had given him for the train, he bought books instead and walked home.[9] His mother, finding the trunk filled with anarchist books, "burned them all."[10]

Čabrinović went one more time to Belgrade, arriving in October 1913. He found a job at the state press. "I worked there with a beginning pay of 90 dinars. I suffered there. It was frightful. I did not want to write home, because I was not on good terms with my father, who even forbade my sisters to write to me. I became desperate. Later they gave me a little raise, but my need was great. I wrote home, but no one wrote back. It was as if to them I was not alive. I am pretty sentimental. Every day I was caught up in more desperate thoughts. In the café *Zirovni* [sic] *Vijenac* [Acorn Wreath] and *Zlatna Moruna* [Golden Sturgeon] I talked in revolutionary terms with people with whom I met at the time."[11] And thus the stars began to align for Čabrinović, guiding him toward his destiny in Sarajevo a few shorts months from then.

He wasn't alone. Another student from Bosnia who moved among the Bosnian diaspora, roomed for a time with Princip, and eventually became the third member of the main troika that plotted Ferdinand's death, was Trifko Grabež. By a strange coincidence, Grabež was born on June 28 (in 1895 in Pale). Although he was the son of a Greek Orthodox priest, Grabež didn't share his father's religious beliefs. Instead, he was a staunch atheist and a Yugoslav nationalist, though he said he acted entirely in Bosnia's interests, not Serbia's.[12] Before his involvement in the conspiracy he had received fourteen days in jail and had been expelled from high school for slapping a pro-Habsburg teacher over the latter's disparaging comments about him. The decisive physicality of this action proved to be a departure from his normal behaviour, because even though he gravitated naturally to like-minded radicals in Belgrade, and was a willing participant in the assassination, he ultimately failed to act when the time came. His role as a participant observer who nevertheless got the same punishment as the assassin made Grabež's fate as pathetic as it was tragic. Princip seemed to have had an inkling that Grabež lacked the stern stuff to be an assassin, at least at that particular moment, because he advised him to save himself for another occasion.[13]

However, Grabež did claim to have come up with the idea of the assassination on his own, though he admitted that Princip did so simultaneously, and that they made the final decision together. Čabrinović's story at the trial was different. He recalled receiving a clipping from a newspaper called *Pokret*, which he identified by the breadth of its print, sent anonymously from somewhere in Habsburg territory and enciphered with the word "Greeting." The clipping announced the arrival of Franz Ferdinand in Sarajevo later that year:

About noon I went to dinner to the Zeleni Vijenac [Green Wreath] and I dined alone. After that I went to the cafe Zirovni Vijenac. There I ordered coffee and read the newspaper. Next to me Princip danced with a

*couple of Bosnians. One was called Mane, and the other Branko. They were
from somewhere in the Krajina. After the dance I remembered the clipping and showed it to Princip. He read it and said nothing to me. I attached
no importance to that communication, although I thought of an assassination. I did not think that communication would play such a significant
role in my life. I put it in my pocket and went out for a walk. In the evening I went out to supper to the Zeleni Vijenac and when I was finished
with supper Princip came. He said to me, "Let's go out and talk about that
report." I realized that Princip was thinking of an assassination....when I
left with Princip we went into the park at Obilić's and there Princip suggested that we two carry out an assassination of the Heir Apparent.*[14]

Čabrinović's story was later supported by Princip who, like
Čabrinović, seemed both to take credit for the idea himself and to
collectivize the effort. The rivalry between the two men is evident
in their description of the order of events.

President [of Jury]: *Tell me now, when did you first learn that the late
    Heir Apparent would come to Sarajevo?*
Princip: *When I came to Belgrade in the month of March I read it in the
    newspapers. I think the German ones.*
President: *Did you then come up with the idea of carrying out an
    assassination?*
Princip: *Yes.*
President: *Was that before you spoke with Cabrinovic [sic]?*
Princip: *Yes, before.*
President: *How long before?*
Princip: *A few days before. Then I talked with him later because I knew
    we were of the same opinions. I said, "How about arranging an assassi-
    nation?"—after which he showed me some newspaper clippings.*[15]

In his interview with Martin Pappenheim in Theresienstadt,
Princip recalled that he spoke "with Chabrinovitch on this matter, who was of the same opinion. Chabrinovitch said he ought

to leave the attempt to him. But he was a type-setter, not of sufficient intelligence. Thought he was not sufficiently nationalist because previously an anarchist and socialist. Said they would both do it."[16]

After a short hesitation that was due, Čabrinović claimed, to his wish to assassinate a "bootlicker" in the Bosnian *Sabor* (Assembly) rather than a personage like Ferdinand, he agreed to the plan.[17] The next significant impediment to the plot was procuring the means of assassination. The assassins decided to contact Serbian *komite* leader Vojislav Tankosić through their Bosnian acquaintance Milan Ciganović (both men were born in villages near Princip's Gornji Obljaj). Tankosić was also a member of the Black Hand, whose high-level military members were in conflict with the Serbian government over whether civilian or military control was to be given priority in the territories Serbia had annexed because of the Balkan Wars. Ciganović approached Tankosić and impressed him about the seriousness of the plot; he was given four Browning pistols, six percussion bombs from the Serbian state arsenal at Kragujevac, as well as cyanide of potassium (to be used by the conspirators once the attempt had been made). The assassins then took some target practice in a quiet back corner of the spacious Košutnjak Park, firing at the trunk of an old oak tree that was shaped like a man.

Tankosić requested a meeting with the young Bosnians before their departure for Sarajevo. Princip, who bitterly remembered Tankosić's rejection when he tried to enlist with the Serbian guerillas, refused to go, and it was eventually decided that Grabež, being more serious than Čabrinović, and liable to make a better impression, would represent the troika.

Tankosić's critical decision to support the assassination wasn't one he would have made on his own. Most likely he consulted the leader of the Black Hand, Dragutin Dimitrijević, nom de guerre "Apis," who had led the assassins of Serbian King Alexander Obrenović and his wife in 1903 (and who carried bullets from the king's guard in his body to the end of his days). According to Cedimir Popović, a former Black Hand Central Committee member, Apis told him that Tankosić had come one day and said some Bosnians had been bothering him about going home, and he asked whether he should let them. Apis naturally didn't want to waste time on the matter, but then Tankosić informed him they were planning "some 'great deed.'"[18] against Ferdinand. This was rather different and got Apis's attention.[19] According to Black Hand historian David Mackenzie, Apis wanted his own seasoned guerrillas to make the attempt rather than some untried Bosnians, but the latter wouldn't hear of it.

In contrast to the assassins' account of the origin of the assassination was Apis's version at his show trial before a Serbian military court at Salonika in 1917. Apis was charged with conspiring to assassinate Serbian Crown Prince Alexander. "I thought that with the removal of the heir to the throne, Ferdinand, the military party and current he headed would lose strength, thus removing or at least delaying the danger of war somewhat. For that purpose I hired [Rade] Malobabić[20] to organize Ferdinand's murder upon his arrival in Sarajevo....Malobabić carried out my instructions, organized and carried through the assassination. Its chief participants were in my service and received small honoraria which I sent to them through Malobabić."[21]

Although Apis knew Serbia needed time to recover from the Balkan Wars, he "also believed only terroristic methods were effective in achieving Serbia's national goals....By uniting South Slavs of the Monarchy under a uniform, co-ordinated administration [trialism], the archduke might halt erosion of Austrian power and envelop Serbia."[22] Removing Ferdinand and thus the threat of trialism would *prevent* an invasion of Serbia! However, the authenticity of Apis's confession is questionable given his very personal motivations; he hoped that by tapping into nationalistic feelings in Serbia, since the country was in the midst of the First World War, he could save himself. He was wrong. Along with his right-hand man, Rade Malobabić, and another defendant, he was executed by an Imperial Serbian firing squad on June 26, 1917.

The debate about the origins of the assassination has never been resolved with any categorical finality. It's natural to conclude that the young Bosnians in the first troika, all still in their teens, were sought out by experienced, powerful men in the Black Hand who were engaged in an ideological conflict with the ruling regime of Serbia. Even if these men hadn't actively searched for the assassins in Belgrade's cafés, the propaganda spread by the *Narodna Odbrana*, which was the ideological backbone of the military tactics they favoured, shaped the assassins' thinking. That said, most historians have tended to accept the young Bosnians' vigorous denials at their trial that someone else came up with the plan for the assassination.

✦ In the afternoon I arrived in Belgrade. Located on the confluence of the Danube and Sava rivers, the city is larger than its Croatian counterpart, Zagreb, but like it, it still bore the plodding architectural mark of communism. Despite this, and the beating it took during NATO bombing in 1999, Belgrade was to me an attractive city with leafy parks of oak and plane trees, trendy shopping promenades, hip cafés, elegant iron-gated mansions, ornate buildings given over to the arts or government, and a river island called Ada Ciganlija (roughly "Gypsy Island"), which is located four kilometres from the confluence and was turned into a recreational zone and fresh water source.

The long beach on Ada Ciganlija, which draws tens of thousands of Belgraders on sweltering days, wasn't on my itinerary, so I made my way to Košutnjak Park, where the conspirators took target practice in 1914. The park is six kilometres from downtown Belgrade, and, because it is wooded and spacious, was the site of other covert, politically motivated violence in the past; in 1868 Mihajlo Obrenović III, prince of Serbia, was assassinated here while on a walk, and in 2000, Ivan Stambolić, former president of Serbia, who was a mentor to Slobodan Milošević but was later betrayed by him in an astonishing Machiavellian political manoeuvre, was kidnapped in the park while jogging, hustled into a white van, shot execution-style, and buried in a pit in northern Serbia.[23]

These doings hardly seem possible in a park with an atmosphere like Košutnjak's. Joggers passed me on the trails that wound through the woods, and I could hear the roar of swimmers from one of the outdoor pools. There was, for me, such a disconnect between the past and the present that I decided to leave and head to another part of the city, where I could better resurrect the ghosts of the past.

Kalemegdan Park is located below the fortress of the same name, which sits on a ridge high atop Belgrade and offers a bird's eye view of New Belgrade to the south, Great War Island in the confluence of the Sava and Danube rivers, and the spacious plains of Pannonia, which stretch hundreds of kilometres to the north. From the fortress, which was built to thwart Ottoman attacks, I entered the narrow streets of the Old Town and walked the groomed pathways of the park itself. It was somewhere here that Princip, Grabež, and their friend Đuro Šarac sat for a photo in May 1914. Civilly attired in suits, ties, and fedoras, they appear serious and thoughtful but otherwise expressionless. Most striking for me is the change in Princip. Gone was the well-fed cherub from the studio photo of 1911, and in his place the grownup, mustachioed assassin whose long travels and years of privation show in his gaunt face. Gone, too, was the book that was present in the 1911 photo, and its absence seemed to signal his shift from literary interests to revolutionary action (though in truth he only stopped reading when he was arrested). The hat pushed back off his high forehead and the crossed legs add a breezy confidence to his demeanour.

In Kalemegdan Park, sitting on opposite ends of a bench like Grabež and Princip, were two elderly men playing chess. Dressed

Trifko Grabež, Đuro Šarac, and Gavrilo Princip in Kalemegdan Park, May 1914.
[from Dedijer, Sarajevo 1914, p. 993]

alike, they wore white, short-sleeved polyester shirts, their under-shirts visible underneath, grey slacks, and sandals. The smaller of the men was silent, while the other, a big guy with a heavy voice, didn't seem to stop talking from the moment I stopped to watch them.

"Canada, huh? I've heard of that place! What are you doing here?" When I told him he asked me my name.

"Hey Dragan, what do you think of this? This guy's a Croat and he's researching Gavrilo Princip!"

"Canadian, actually," I corrected him.

"Doesn't matter. Your father was born there, so you're a Croat."

"Sure," I said.

He embarked on an enthusiastic lecture, explaining who Gavrilo Princip was, whereabouts he lived in Belgrade, and what he had done when he was here. He claimed Princip had joined the Black Hand in 1913, which wasn't true, and that he'd fought the Turks in the Balkan Wars (wrong again). But what struck me as true was his unbounded enthusiasm for his own nation and its past. His enthusiasm was honestly held, but it was the very thing Croats liked to mock (though they were basically guilty of such jingoism, as well). Not far into his history lesson he soared, and he took me with him. I tingled with enthusiasm and sympathy for this misunderstood and oppressed people. There were few practical hints to trouble the magic current of phrases unless his decisive comments about "exterminating the *Šiptare*" (Albanians) in Kosovo were considered.

As he spoke his thick hands moved about to emphasize his words, and I noticed some turquoise numbers tattooed on his left forearm. They were roughly hewn as though cut by someone holding a penknife in his fist. When I asked about them, he told me they signified the unit he was part of in the Second World War. I don't know why, maybe because he seemed to swallow the words then, but I doubted his honesty and thought a wish of his had turned at some point into a reality.

His silent friend lifted a knight to draw his attention, waved it around and placed it dramatically on its new spot.

"Look at him," my friend said, "he thinks he's got me." He went over to consider his options.

I asked them what they did when they weren't here.

Dragan, the silent one, suddenly piped up. "He'll do nothing. He'll come to my place and drink my beer and eat the food my wife makes for him. What else is there for him? He's alone at home now."

My friend looked down at the chessboard, still studying his next move. His natural talkativeness had left him. I took this as my cue to go, so I asked permission to take a photo of them, shook both their hands and went on my way.[24]

✦ The next morning I set off for Bosnia. I followed the direction of the assassins, who left Belgrade on May 28. It took them eight days and nights to reach Sarajevo, covering most of the ground on foot in an effort to evade both Serbian and Austrian police. Their underground route was what Major Tankosić had called the *kanal*, or channel, which Čabrinović interpreted foolishly as an actual underground tunnel to Bosnia. While I drove in the comfort of my car, they had plodded through rain and mud, with bombs tied around their waists, revolvers, ammunition, and cyanide in their pockets.

The first leg of their journey was by boat to Šabac, fifty kilometres west of Belgrade on the Sava River. Because the conspirators had to wait for a local captain to arrange their secret crossing of the border at Loznica, they visited a nearby spa to relax. Čabrinović's imprudence and unsuitability for serious revolutionary action was on show from the start when he started to chat with a *komite* soldier who noticed the bombs around his waist and wondered where he was going. While Princip managed to get Čabrinović out of this fix and later tried to cover his own tracks by sending a postcard to his cousin, on which he said he would be visiting a monastery to study for an exam, Čabrinović persisted in his careless ways; he wrote to some friends, quoting a heroic Serbian folk poem about the first uprising against the Turks in 1804, and he provocatively wrote on another postcard, "A good horse and a hero will always find the best way to break through."[25]

The argument that flared up between Čabrinović and his two fellow assassins, which Princip at the trial would call a spat between friends, caused a serious rift on the journey to Sarajevo. Princip stood toe to toe with his larger, explosive friend and ordered him to return his weapons and travel on his own to Tuzla by way of the frontier town of Zvornik. Evidently, it didn't occur to him that Čabrinović on his own could be more problematic than Čabrinović supervised, but their being found out with the weapons was probably his greatest worry. Čabrinović was angered and hurt by this autocratic decision (Grabež's assent made it seem more democratic than it really was), but he agreed to meet them at Tuzla.

The two remaining conspirators slogged on from Šabac with three bombs around their waists and two revolvers in their pockets. They spent most of May 30 at a frontier post run by Sergeant-major Rade Grbić. Princip wiled the lazy afternoon away with more target practice, shooting a hawk on a tree. The next day they arrived on a wooded island in the Drina called Isakovića Ada. One of Grbić's official duties was to prevent smuggling, but the island also served the Black Hand as a covert post for intelligence reports out of Bosnia. The cover for these activities was an illegal bar that sold cheap šljivovica to Bosnians who easily crossed the ford from the Bosnian side. When Grabež and Princip arrived on the island, they had to wait for a young man called Mićo Mićić (a former baker turned peasant who had served a twenty-one-day sentence for hitting a man with a bottle) who was asked to go to Bosnia and bring back middle-aged peasant, smuggler, and Black Hand courier Jakov Milović, their guide into Bosnian territory. Young Mićić had better things to do that day; he had planned to take a girl to a dance, but he agreed to find Milović. The sergeant also warned him to keep his mouth shut about what he'd seen if he wanted to keep his head. If Mićić had been threatened, why then, wondered the judge at the trial in Sarajevo, had he gone back to the island? Said Mićić, "The devil made me do it. That's my bad luck."[26] Asked a second time, he answered, "I returned. I had not finished my brandy."[27]

The next leg of the journey for Princip and Grabež was a twenty-one-hour haul into Bosnia beginning on the night of June 1. They followed Milović through forests and over plowed fields as a storm swept in. Tired and wet, the assassins asked to stop at a peasant hut, where they hoped to find someone to help carry the revolvers and bombs. Milović led them to the home of a friend, Obren Milošević, who offered them a roof, Turkish coffee, and a bag for the weapons. When it was learned that Mićić had disappeared into the night, Milošević and Milović agreed to help with the transportation. For their troubles, Mićić and Milošević were arrested after the assassination but eventually released because the judge believed Princip and Grabež's testimony that they had threatened the peasants with violence. At the trial Princip said he had told Milošević, "'You can't tell anyone that we have passed, otherwise your house will be destroyed.'" Princip added, "Those words were not intended seriously. I did not believe that anything would happen to them. I knew that it would work on him when he was threatened."[28] For his involvement, Milović was sentenced to hang but was reprieved by imperial pardon and sentenced to twenty years' imprisonment. He succumbed to tuberculosis and malnutrition in 1916. A poor peasant widower, he left behind four children.

As I stood watching the Drina slide past, I thought of similar rolling, wooded terrain I had explored in Croatia, and I understood better what endurance, tenacity, and zeal it had taken to transport the weapons to Sarajevo and ultimately kill Ferdinand. Princip would have walked across the far ends of the earth to pull the trigger. The single-mindedness of it all now gave me pause. What's more, it was obvious that this cloak and dagger operation was amateurish, hastily planned, and implicated far more people than necessary. No thought was given at the time to the serious consequences for the peasants who, despite sharing Princip's political views, paid a heavy price for their patriotism. So, I wondered, was this still the logical end-point of the nationalism shown by the chess player in Belgrade? In my mind the road to Sarajevo was westward, where the sun set, and toward death.

What, though, did the assassins feel as they trudged along? Hans Koning in his novel about the assassination has Princip describe his feelings this way:

> It was a green walk. The vast, friendly forests of our Bosnia were all around us and over us. Trees, bushes, leaves, grass, and even the water we waded through was green, was ours, and the slashing rain was green and not inimical. I saw us as if from an imaginary height, two tiny figures moving along this huge earth, protected by that early summer canopy of nature. Can you imagine being too weary to take another step and at the same time feeling intensely and superiorly alive?...Nothing else existed or mattered. And within that present we were magically happy.[29]

4 ✦ VIŠEGRAD, FOČA

✦ EASTERN HAUNTS

IN JUNE 2006, accompanied by my father again, I travelled through the eastern sector of Bosnia-Herzegovina, which is part of its Republika Srpska, or Serbian Republic. Since the assassins walked through here on their road to Tuzla, the demographic makeup of the area has changed considerably, as much of the Muslim population was ethnically cleansed during the war of the 1990s.

We drove east from Sarajevo, past the former Bosnian-Serb stronghold of Pale, where former Bosnian-Serb leader Radovan Karadžić once held court, and through wooded, hilly country. It was a drizzly, grey day and the clouds hung low over the hills. The new glistening road snuck through one valley after another, past sparsely populated hamlets and flat green meadows dotted with sheep. As we were passing through another little valley, we saw a chapel on the side of the road and on its back stairs some sheep crowding under the roof out of the rain. They stood there, patiently miserable, waiting out the shower. Although they watched me in silence, the moment I snapped a picture and turned back to the car they began to bleat loudly. They continued bleating as I shut the door and put the camera away.

"They didn't like you there," my father laughed.

"No, but they waited to tell me. Such cowards!"

"The thought took a while!" He turned in the direction of the street that led to the hamlet. "Look, you should talk to her."

I saw an old baba making her way slowly toward us. She wore a poppy-red suit jacket, grey skirt, dress shoes, and a freshly pressed white kerchief. An umbrella protected her from the rain and a cigarette dangled deftly out of her toothless mouth. Once up close I saw that the cardigan under her jacket was missing buttons and was closed by a safety pin instead. It was a weekend, so she was dressed up and headed to the local store for cigarettes.

We got to talking about her life in the village. "Oohhhhh, itsh not shuch a eeshy life as it youshed a be," she mumbled, shaking her head sadly. Because of her missing teeth and the cigarette that wobbled between her toothless gums it was almost impossible to understand her. From what we were able to figure out, she lived with her daughter and her two children. The two men were long gone, in fact most of the men in the area were gone, including the old woman's husband, who went mad and disappeared during the war (she still wore her wedding band, however). She said her daughter was unemployed and that they could barely live off her own miserly pension. The daughter had been out the night before, and was just getting up now (it was close to noon). As the old woman went on, she got progressively more upset, her voice cracking at times and tears welling up in her eyes.

After a bit of convincing, she agreed to pose for a photograph. By the time I'd fetched the camera the cigarette was gone, her

> *Sheep on church steps near Pale.*

mouth had closed and her body had gone as stiff as a mannequin. The photo, I realized, wouldn't have much life to it. I asked her her name, but she didn't want to tell me. She'd had enough of us, so she waved goodbye and walked down the road to the store.

In the car again, I wondered what had made her so forthcoming.

"Maybe she wanted money," my father suggested.

"Could be," I agreed. "We should have given her some."

"Maybe." He stopped to think for a second. "But she had enough for cigarettes."

I drove off, pleased with this first "adventure" of the day. Again, I recalled my Croatian friends' fear-mongering about Bosnia, and I smiled to myself. My mood was short-lived, however, because only a few hundred metres farther on, a police-man suddenly stepped onto the road and waved us down. He approached the car slowly. "*Dobar dan*," he said cheerfully, bending to speak through our open window. "Where are you going today?"

"To Višegrad," I answered curtly.

"To Višegrad." Without prompting, he gave us directions, tell-ing us the road ahead had been closed for repairs but was open again, so we should avoid the detour to the right. He asked to see our map, pointing out where we were supposed to go. His help-fulness made me wary for some reason. A few seconds later his partner emerged from the patrol car and approached us. This guy was less cheery. I could see his fat pistol against his heavy hip. He held up a pad of paper, which looked like a ticket book and said, "You were speeding."

"Not a chance," I told him categorically.

The two policemen looked at each, and the one with the ticket tried again. "The radar says you were speeding. The radar doesn't lie." He shrugged to excuse himself from blame.

< *Old woman in a village near Pale.*

They took our passports, registration, insurance, and car rental agreement.

My father chose that moment to get out and argue with them. I sat stiffly in my seat, thinking we really ought to have paid up and left. I wondered vaguely what my wife would have thought now.

When my father began peering into the patrol car for the radar, the second officer suddenly tried a different tack. "Could you open the trunk?"

Once my father did, he asked him to remove our bags, and he cast a glance around. In a loud, self-satisfied voice he proclaimed, "You have no first aid kit."

"Oh, come on," I piped up from my seat. "That's ridiculous. We rented this car; how were we supposed to know that we needed a first aid kit in Bosnia. You can't blame us for that."

The officer shrugged and returned to his car to write up the ticket.

A beat up Yugo puttered past, its occupants gawking at us.

"Are you saying they have a first aid kit?" I asked.

"Every car has one. In Bosnia it is the law," the first policeman declared piously.

"Look," said my father. "We're not bad people. We're just going about our business."

"Are you saying we're bad people?"

"Don't answer that," I told my father in English.

He didn't. Instead he began to poke around the back seats. From the pocket behind the passenger seat he pulled out a first aid kit and held it aloft like a trophy.

The officers were disappointed. They conferred for a moment then informed us that we didn't have a *trikot*, the triangular reflector you put on the road behind your car when you're changing a tire.

My father was at a loss. The trunk was empty, nor was there anything in the other compartments. Again the second officer went back to his patrol car to write up a ticket. Then my father was inspired, and he lifted the spare tire in the trunk and pulled out the red *trikot*. The second policeman, who had hastily written up a ticket, now turned in confusion to his partner and asked what they should do. They moved out of hearing, then came back and told us we didn't have a set of spare headlights.

We looked at them, and they looked at us, and then we started to laugh. All four of us. Pulling out his wallet, my father informed them of my purpose in Bosnia. He said readers in Canada would certainly be interested in how the Bosnian police did business. Gratuitously, I reminded them of Bulwer-Lytton's saying, "The pen is mightier than the sword." (He might have responded with the self-complimentary Serb stereotype, that in a conflict with authority the Serb reaches for his sword while the Croat reaches for his pen.)

The cheerful policeman who had approached the car first shook his head and wagged his finger. "No, don't write about this." He explained that they were obliged to fill their quota of fifteen tickets a day, or face being docked pay. If this happened more than twice they could be fined or even lose their jobs. They seemed genuinely sympathetic about fleecing their fellow Bosnians, most of whom were much poorer than we were.

"How do you think it feels," the second cop asked, "to hand out a ticket to a guy who has to work a week to pay it? I know his situation all too well. I have two kids at home. In the end it's either the other guy or me."

So on this last note about the policing system in Bosnia, my father handed him forty Bosnian marks[1] (around thirty-five dollars), and we headed toward Goražde on our way to Višegrad. By that point we'd forgotten the first cop's instructions, and when we hit a fork in the road, both directions paved, we wavered about which to take. The one to the right seemed to point south, where Goražde lay. Had we looked at the map we would have known better, but we weren't thinking straight after our last encounter.

At first the paved road led promisingly toward the first range of hills, but a few kilometres on it changed its mind, turned to dirt, and corkscrewed narrowly up into thickly forested hills, cresting

Goražde.

from time to time before it climbed once more. No cars passed us on the way down, and there was no sign of life anywhere. Yet the road pressed ahead doggedly as though it really did have a place to go.

After twenty minutes, we passed a small meadow slashed into the side of the slanting forest where three brown cows were grazing. They seemed to have dropped from the sky. Who had brought them here? Where did their owners live? We drove on and on and saw no one. Only much later when we entered the clouds did we come across an old man walking on the side of the road. He wore a ski parka and an unfriendly expression, and his mad eyes stared at our passing car as though he had never seen one before. His tiny brick house was farther on, just below the road, and in the yard an elderly woman was pouring boiling water into a rusty barrel. Most likely she was making preparations to slaughter a pig or some chickens. The steam from the barrel rose into the cool, grey air to join the low, torn wisps of clouds that hung over the hills.

Finally the road began to descend as diaphanous shafts of sun lit the orange roofs in the valleys. Goražde glittered far below us along a curve of the emerald-coloured Drina River. It was a beautiful sight from so high up as it must have been for Bosnian-Serb forces who laid siege to the city during the war (they shelled it despite its Serbian population and its status as a UN safe haven).[2] Shabby, one-storey buildings snaked in long rows along the streets. A few were newly painted, but most had a dull, weathered appearance, with a few bullets holes as a reminder of hostilities. Young guys drove past on mopeds, and older men sat on the low wall and steps leading down to the grassy banks of the Drina, which sparkled in the sun and gave off a cool, clean air.

We stayed just long enough to fill up the gas tank and visit the washroom. I laughed when my father went in and found a rusty faucet jutting out of the wall at knee-level beside the iron basin instead of toilet paper. He had no choice but to squat on the treads and wipe himself afterwards with his bare hand. He came out shaking off water, and said, "It's alright, no problem."

"Don't eat with your left hand," I suggested as we drove off.

"Will do."

✦ The drive northeast to Višegrad took us along the Drina, which winds narrowly between very steep hills and then opens at other times into small lakes. There are inlets cleft into high, jagged cliffs, shacks on the far bank with small motorboats for fishing, and on the peaks of the hills are tiny meadows where we could see houses.

The road passed through some dozen tunnels, many with Cyrillic names engraved on the concrete entrances. Most used to have lights but the bulbs had burned out long ago, and while some had concrete ceilings, others were made of rock. This morning near Pale, we'd passed through a tunnel even more basic than the ones here. We waited for the green light to tell us all was clear before driving into the darkness. The low ceiling was entirely of

The bridge on the Drina at Višegrad.

rock, and fat drops of water splattered regularly against the windshield.

Before we knew it, we passed through the last of the tunnels and came upon the famous Višegrad bridge. It was ordered built by a vizier named Mehmed Paša Sokollu (Sokolović), born to the Sokolović family in eastern Bosnia, who had been wrested from his home as a child by the Turks as part of their *devşirme* programme, but who never forgot his origins. Perhaps because I'd read Ivo Andrić's novel *The Bridge on the Drina* years ago, the bridge in my imagination was larger and more grandiose than it was in reality, but it was still a remarkable sight in the middle of this rugged landscape. In another story about a different bridge, "The Bridge on the Žepa," Andrić captured this feeling: "[T]he landscape could not fit itself to the bridge, nor the bridge to the landscape. Seen from the side, the white span of its bold arch always looked isolated and lonely and took the traveler by surprise, like a strange thought gone astray and caught among crags in the wilderness."[3]

The bridge at Višegrad no longer had the same effect described by Andrić, not only because it had changed over time but also because it was set against a town that served as its main background, not the wilderness. As can be expected of a structure completed in 1571, the bridge was showing its age; it was cracked and stained in places, and what was once white limestone had turned a dull greyish or cream colour depending on the light conditions. Yet somehow its surroundings made it shine all the more; a weedy garbage-strewn lane ran along the far bank and many of the houses were gutted or pockmarked by bullets. The dirty streets were empty of people. Even the centre of the town, where a number of café–restaurants crowded around a cul de sac, had a sad, depressed air. It was hard to imagine this ghost town as it once was, "an attractive, largely Muslim village surrounded by evergreen forests."[4]

We sat outside for a meal at one of the cafés. The waiter, a big, bullet-headed man neatly clothed in white shirt and black

pants trod heavily across the cement floor to our table. I thought
his attire incongruous with the rundown surroundings, but he
wanted to keep up appearances. The owner had tried to do the
same with his place; the steps into the bar, I noticed, as well as
the bar itself and the frame of the open window, were newly built
out of wood. The waiter's accent told us he was a Serb, and he took
our order with curt unfriendliness. Later, he bumped the empty
steel chair at our table with his feet while bringing the oil and vin-
egar, and did it again serving our meal. As I ate, I could see him
inside talking quietly to another man, who turned away when I
caught his eye.

The *ražnići* we'd ordered, veal shish-kebabs on wooden skewers,
were the best I'd eaten in the former Yugoslavia.

"Don't eat with your left hand," I reminded my father.

"It's okay," he replied. "It's dry now."

While we ate I noticed cars arriving from the main drag, honking and then departing. Most of the drivers were young men who
wanted to check out the "action" downtown. A few older guys
arrived at our café, greeted the ones inside, and then sat on the
terrace. A man showed up at the café next door, the one with three
Karlovačko umbrellas (the name of a Croatian beer), said hello to the
lone guest, an older fellow reading a newspaper, but never looked
this way. Nor did our guys acknowledge them. It was as though
they were invisible to each other.

I asked our waiter who the men were next door and he
answered, lowering his voice and shrugging, "*To su Muslimani*."[5] He
pocketed our money and returned to the bar.

On that note we took a stroll on Višegrad's bridge. The sun was
out and a gentle breeze ruffled the surface of the smooth, oil-like
surface of the slow-moving Drina. In the middle of the bridge the
air was suddenly fresh and cool. I saw a pair of swallows skim
over the water and pass through one of the bridge's arches. Even
though the bridge's stone was pocked in places, eaten by time,
it still gave me a pleasant feeling, a feeling of separation from

the shabbiness and bad atmosphere of the town. I thought of the untold conversations that had occurred on the stone porch: lovers huddled against cool evenings; Orthodox priests, their robes sustained gently by the morning air, off on some business; the coffee-makers with their vessels and Turkish cups and coal braziers; the Turkish janissaries of the Ottoman era; and the *Schwabe* of the Austro-Hungarian occupation. I went further back, to the beginnings, when the white arches first rose above the green river. According to local legend, Andrić writes, the fairy of the boatmen had hindered the bridge's building,

> as always and everywhere there is something to hinder building, destroying by night what had been built by day, until 'something' had whispered from the waters and counselled Rade the Mason to find two infant children, twins, brother and sister, named Stoja and Ostoja, and wall them into the central pier of the bridge. A reward was promised to whoever found them and brought them hither. At last the guards found such twins, still at the breast, in a distant village and the Vezir's men took them away by force; but when they were taking them away, their mother would not be parted from them and, weeping and wailing, insensible to blows and to curses, stumbled after them as far as Višegrad itself, where she succeeded in forcing her way to Rade the Mason. The children were walled into the pier, for it could not be otherwise, but Rade, they say, had pity on them and left openings in the pier through which the unhappy mother could feed her sacrificed children. Those are the finely carved blind windows, narrow as loopholes, in which the wild doves now nest. In memory of that, the mother's milk has flowed from those walls for hundreds of years. That is the thin white stream which, at certain times of year, flows from that faultless masonry and leaves an indelible mark on the stone....Men scrape those milky traces off the piers and sell them as medical powder to women who have no milk after giving birth.[6]

The Višegrad bridge, like the one in Mostar, has served as a metaphor for ethnic harmony in Bosnia. In my more optimistic moments, I find myself in agreement. If hatred were so entrenched, wouldn't people have been at each other's throats for centuries, and wouldn't ethnically pure communities have developed long ago? But some historians have noted that the concept of peaceful social relations in Bosnia was mainly a product of urban intellectuals in Sarajevo, who influenced foreign commentators.[7] For Noel Malcolm, these writers who have portrayed Bosnia as a "wonderland of permanent inter-religious harmony have over-reacted. But a closer inspection of history will show that the animosities which did exist were not absolute and unchanging. Nor were they the inevitable consequences of the mixing together of different religious communities. The main basis of hostility [prior to the rise of nationalism in the late nineteenth century] was not ethnic or religious but economic: the resentment felt by the members of a mainly (but not exclusively) Christian peasantry towards their Muslim landowners."[8]

What did Ivo Andrić himself believe? While *The Bridge on the Drina* depicts a measure of social tolerance, and seems to reject the rising pan-Serb chauvinism of the late nineteenth century, his work as a whole is darkly pessimistic about Bosnia's social mosaic and tends to present the animosity between different communities as profoundly ingrained.[9] In his novel *The Woman from Sarajevo* he suggests that people of different faiths hate one another from birth to death, senselessly and deeply. Often they will spend their whole lives without finding a moment to express that hatred in all its facets. And in *Bosnian Chronicle*, a character says the following:

Four faiths live in this narrow, mountainous and meagre strip of land. Each of them is exclusive and strictly separate from the others. You all live under one sky and from the same soil, but the centre of spiritual life of each of these four groups is far away, in a foreign land, in Rome, Moscow, Istanbul, Mecca, Jerusalem and God alone knows where, but at any rate not here where the people are born and die. And each group considers that its well-being is conditioned by the disadvantage of each of the other three faiths, and that they can make progress only at their cost. Each of them has made

intolerance the greatest virtue. And each of them is expecting salvation
from somewhere outside, each from the opposite direction.[10]

Although this observer is a foreigner, he echoes sentiments
about Bosnia's internal dynamics, which are evident throughout
Andrić's work. In "Story from 1920," the speaker notes the nightly
tolling from Christian bell towers and the call to prayer from the
mosque and the silent calculations of time in the Sephardic and
Ashkenazic systems. "And thus even during the night, the difference which divides these sleeping beings has been emphasized,
beings who will, when they rise, rejoice and mourn, entertain
and fast, according to their four different hostile calendars, and
who will send all their wishes and prayers up to one heaven in
four different church languages. And this difference, sometimes
openly and visibly, sometimes invisibly and basely, approaches
hatred, often identifying with it."[11]

Višegrad's bridge was used during the last war as a stage for
these hatreds. In the spring of 1992, hundreds of Muslims were
herded onto the bridge and along the riverbanks, murdered and
dumped into the Drina, turning its green waters red. Others
were forced into buildings and incinerated alive. Brutal rapes of
Muslim women and various sadistic acts (including one case of
a man being dragged around town by car) occurred in Višegrad.
The Muslim presence here was reduced to virtually nil during the
war as a local Serbian warlord named Milan Lukić and his "White
Eagle" paramilitaries, along with local Serbs and police, carried out a vicious pogrom, an early example of ethnic cleansing
in Bosnia.[12] This was a theatre of overwhelming cruelty, which
had nothing to do with the more pragmatic reasons for fighting
over Višegrad (such as its location near a hydroelectric dam on the
Drina, or its strategic position on the road between Belgrade to the
east, Sarajevo to the west, and Herzegovina to the southwest).

The shattering of the ideal symbolized by the Višegrad bridge
was important to my travels through Bosnia because it appeared

to be the extreme culmination of the nationalistic passions under-lying the assassination in 1914. No doubt, the young assassins who trudged through the woods north of here were enthusiastic Serbs. But, as they stated at the investigation and the trial, they conceived of the assassination as a political and symbolic act that would lead to the unification of all South Slavs within a Yugoslav federation, and their youthful idealism wouldn't have allowed for extreme expressions of Serbian nationalism against fellow South Slavs. Princip and most young Bosnians would have considered ethnic cleansing an egregious crime. One might even argue that, among Serbs generally at the time, the idea of a greater Serbia was rendered harmless because it was understood in the Serbian imagination as, what John Allcock calls, a mainly metaphysical space "defined by points of symbolic reference such as Kosovo and the monasteries of Fruška Gora."[13] The question today is whether or not, despite these claims, a mainline through the rest of Serbdom runs directly and bloodily from Gavrilo Princip to Milan Lukić and his ilk. In other words, is there a direct link conceptu-ally between Princip's Serb-led Yugoslavism to its incarnation in the first days of the war in the 1990s, when the Yugoslav National Army (JNA) entered ethnically conflicted areas allegedly to keep peace, but ostensibly to entrench Serbian gains, and then finally to the ethnic cleansing operations throughout Bosnia? Plenty of non-Serbs in Bosnia would answer with a categorical yes, and those in the know would point out that Princip's generation can-not escape entirely unscathed from accusations of extreme Serbian nationalism.[14] Consider the poisonous memorandum titled "The Expulsion of the Albanians," penned by one of the would-be assas-sins in Sarajevo, Vaso Čubrilović, which began by citing Hitler's and Stalin's successes in expelling Jews and others as examples for Serbia to emulate when it came to the ethnic cleansing of Albanians from Kosovo.[15]

As I stood on the bridge, my conviction about the assassins' self-sacrificial idealism and honourable motivations, with which

I began this journey, was starting to waver. I wondered whether Princip himself would have sacrificed his Yugoslavism for Serbian nationalism if push came to shove? Were they always, unbeknownst to him at the start, one and the same thing? I had no definitive answers to these questions, but from the Višegrad bridge forward, a number of doubts hung over me darkly as I continued my journey.

✦ We drove south to Foča. The road wound unhurriedly through more hilly, almost mountainous, terrain. It was late afternoon, and the sun managed to filter down into the darkly shaded valleys. I imagined the forests in the winter, heavily laden with snow, silent; out of these dense woods the howl of wolves could be heard. From time to time we came across people walking along the road on their way to or from a local store. At one point we saw a chestnut mare pacing back and forth at the end of a rope and a little barefoot kid watching over it from a shack. Generally, though, there were few people and few settlements. This was a beautiful, quiet area removed from the eyes of outsiders.

After a very slow drive on a narrow road behind yet another ancient truck that spewed smoke as it farted up steep grades, we arrived in Foča. A sign[16] directed us off the main road and over a modern bridge that spanned the Drina. An unexceptional town awaited us on the other side, with a main drag made of square, Yugo-era buildings and some cafés pumping out the usual Europop where the town's young men drank and smoked. But unlike dour Višegrad, Foča, tucked neatly in a small valley as it was, with trees everywhere, appeared vibrant and healthy.

Formerly a mainly Muslim town, now almost exclusively Serb, it allegedly harboured numerous indicted war criminals, as well as an energetic hatred for Muslims. But not to worry, a recent travel guide to Bosnia-Herzegovina assured me, "no one will bite your head off....Avoid a history discussion or lecture if possible."[17]

We went in search of some locals to interview. After some time we came across an old man stacking wood against the wall of his house. His brown woollen cap, grey suit, and white shirt buttoned at the collar, gave him the look of a gentleman farmer. Every blade of grass was shaven to the same length, and his backyard, where there was a barn, chicken coop, doghouse, and smoke house, was impeccably tidy. Even the black schnauzer looking alertly at us seemed to have been groomed recently.

I stood at the edge of his yard and explained who I was and my purpose in coming to Bosnia. I was quite conscientious about being polite, reasonable, and friendly so I could get him to talk. I ended with the noble sentiment that I hoped to tell the story of Bosnia from the point of view of everyone, Muslims, Croats, and Serbs. After I'd finished, he put his hand up to his ear and said, "What?"

I repeated myself, more loudly this time. Then I asked him what life was like in Foča. Enthusiastically he answered, "*dobar!*" "good!" Then he went back to piling the wood, leaning over painstakingly as he placed each piece carefully in its spot.

I tried another tack, asking him about the history of Foča, its ethnic makeup and so on. In the middle of the question, he cut me off, pointed toward the house and told me there were men inside who knew all about Foča's history. He had dashed off this suggestion without looking up and went on stacking his wood.

I didn't take his advice because I knew that these men would be as unreceptive as the old man. As I was about to leave I threw out another question, though I knew getting something out of him was hopeless. "What about the Muslims?" I asked. This turned out to be the right question after all because he stood upright, eyes shining brightly, and skidded his one hand against the other. A sharp slap emphasized his words. "*Pobegli su!*" (They ran away!) He smiled broadly and let out a loud laugh. It was infectious, and I laughed, too. What there was to laugh about I didn't know, of course. But I was grateful to him because he'd told me a lot in just a few words. The old man ignored us from then on as he turned his back and went on piling his wood.

It was our cue to go, so we walked around for a while until we encountered some German SFOR peacekeepers stationed in Foča. They were happy to see us, maybe because I spoke German and had German ancestry (my mother and grandmother were born in Kiel). One was a veteran in Bosnia, while the other was newly arrived. Their commander had been stationed the longest there, so they suggested we meet him, but when he spoke to me by cell phone, asking in friendly tones who we were and what we wanted, he forbade his men to bring us there but permitted them to go for coffee.

The elder German was tight-lipped, though cheerful, while the younger was more forthcoming. On the way to the café, I was able to talk with him as his partner went ahead with my father. Even though he'd only been here nine days, the impressions of the place were already there, raw, not filtered by too much protocol. He told me in a hushed voice about the Muslim women who had been beheaded on the bridge and dumped into the Drina. I learned of others who had been raped by Serbs during the war and had returned to Foča to mount a plaque on the building where they were attacked; they were harassed and threatened by a mob of Serb men, some identified as rapists, who forced them to leave before they put up the plaque. "People here are very passionate and stubborn about their beliefs," the German whispered diplomatically.

In 1992, this passion turned Foča into a violent, lawless place. According to one report at the time, "Gangs of gun-toting Serbs rule Foča, turning the once quiet town into a nightmare landscape of burning streets and houses. The motley assortment of fierce-looking bearded men carry Kalashnikovs and bandoliers or have hand guns tucked into their belts. Some are members of paramilitary groups from Serbia, self-proclaimed crusaders against Islam and defenders of the Serb nation, others are wild-eyed local men, hostile towards strangers and happy to have driven out their Muslim neighbours. No one seems to be in command, and ill-disciplined and bad-tempered gunmen stop and detain people at will."[18]

The young German said the residents of Foča didn't feel guilty about these events because they felt that their lives had been threatened by extreme Muslim fundamentalists. It was an idea that had filtered down to the grassroots level and taken on a dark reality unencumbered by actual facts. One of the men fundamentally responsible for crafting this idea, and the psychotic programme of evil that ensued, former Bosnian-Serb leader and war criminal Radovan Karadžić, was known to have found haven in the area around Foča and all of eastern Republika Srpska. For many years after being indicted in 1995 by the War Crimes Tribunal for the Former Yugoslavia, he managed to elude capture by NATO forces through the help of local people, Mafiosi, and the Greek Orthodox Church. When pressure was brought to bear, he apparently retreated to isolated monasteries high in the mountains, shaving his trademark pompadour and disguising himself as an Orthodox monk. His success in eluding capture was not entirely due to his ingenuity or local support but also to the disinterested engagement of NATO forces reluctant to lose personnel in a firefight with Karadžić's guards (though occasionally raids on his alleged hideouts took place, often spearheaded by American and German forces).[19]

In our chat with the peacekeepers, we didn't cover any of this. Instead we talked about their more prosaic duties, such as assisting in testing freshwater sources, and we talked about other matters like the chances of the German national team in the World Cup. As we walked to the car, I took a last look at Foča. I noticed a road that dawdled into the wooded hills.

"This is a nice place for a run," I remarked.

"Oh yes," the older German answered, "but the commander has prohibited us from running now. The traffic, you know."

5 ✦ DOBOJ, TUZLA

✦ PARCEL PICKUP AND DELIVERY

IN JUNE 2006, my father and I drove east across Croatia's
Slavonia region on the former highway of Brotherhood and Unity
(which once again connected Zagreb and Belgrade), then headed
south into Bosnia-Herzegovina at Slavonski Brod. Our destina-
tion was Tuzla, where the assassins met after splitting up at the
Serbian border, and where they unloaded their weapons before
completing the final leg of their trip to Sarajevo by train.

A cold rain was lashing the dark morning when we arrived
on the Bosnian side, which was marked off unceremoniously by
a few pylons and a shack. Past roads signs in Cyrillic, and roofless gutted houses blackened by fire, which dotted the country
like big gravestones, we entered rolling farm country. There were
plum orchards everywhere, signs advertising *šljivovica*, haystacks
with tires attached to their poles to keep down the plastic sheets,
and occasionally Greek Orthodox churches, newly constructed.

Although there were settlements, the area had always been sparsely populated. There really wasn't much to fight over, yet there had been plenty of killing here.

We soon arrived in Doboj, a town at the confluence of the Usora and Bosna. Besides the thirteenth-century fortress on the hill, fortified by the Ottomans in the fifteenth, there was little of interest to see. The centre of town was ploddingly block-like in style, reminding me of Knin as it looked during my visit in 1999. Only some of the side streets with their tall, venerable trees and old houses saved Doboj from an aesthetic point of view, as though the urban planners of the Yugo period had not gotten around to working on that part of town.

Our first contact with the locals was brief, discourteous, and rather revealing. Again, it gave us a taste of the former Yugoslavia. We went into a bank to convert our euros to the Bosnian currency, the convertible mark, and were served by a sullen clerk who resented having to stop chatting with her co-worker. Her hair was dyed bright mauve, and whatever she did, she did while holding a cigarette between her painted nails (mauve to match her hair). All four clerks were smoking, and the whole room was draped by a suffocating grey cloud stirred lazily by two useless ceiling fans. Even though we came in talking English, my father addressed her in Serbo-Croatian. But she refused to speak to us, just moved the pen with exaggerated slowness over the line where I was to sign my name.

We got out of there and went to eat lunch. The restaurant was relatively elegant by Doboj's standards, with leather chairs, wine-red carpets, a small fountain, and newspapers on wooden racks. Our waiter was a young Serb who sported a spiffy goatee, spoke English well, and told us it was too late for him to leave Doboj. This defeatism didn't seem to square with his bouncy energy. When I asked him how life stood here today he replied, "Doboj had a better spirit before. Outsiders came in and that has changed the atmosphere."

My first reaction to his words was one of pleasant surprise; here was someone who didn't toe the ethnic line but placed value instead on old friendships with Muslims rather than on new ones with fellow Serbs who had arrived after the town's ethnic cleansing. It was only a few weeks later, when I came across a UNHCR report announcing the resettlement of thousands of Muslims to the Doboj region that I wondered whether he was in fact more of a Serbian nationalist than I'd believed.

At any rate, he also informed me that Doboj's old railway station, where the weapons were deposited in 1914, was long gone. There remained little for us to see in Doboj, so we drove on toward Tuzla. It was in Tuzla where the young assassins planned to meet after splitting up at the Bosnian-Serb border. Before Princip and Grabež arrived, they first passed through the village of Priboj where their next contact, a teacher called Veljko Čubrilović, who also happened to be the older brother of young Vaso (member of the second troika), was expecting them. The elder Čubrilović was riding his horse alongside the parish priest and was on the way to a funeral when the two peasants assisting the boys met him. Čubrilović excused himself from the priest's company, pretending to be worried about the flooded road ahead (at which the priest laughed, called him a coward, and went on). Princip and Grabež emerged from the bushes where they'd been hiding, paid the peasants five crowns, warned them to keep silent, and sent them home.

While Princip had been careful about concealing his purpose in going to Sarajevo, and had argued with Čabrinović about his "unrevolutionary" lapses, he was open with Čubrilović. "He kept pestering us the whole time with questions," Princip recalled at the trial. "I don't know how it came about that we told him that we were going to Sarajevo. He said something and then he asked us whether we were going to carry out an assassination. We said that we would. I don't remember which of us said it, but I incidentally told him, that although he had conducted himself in a

completely friendly way that nevertheless we would destroy everything if he said anything."[1] At the trial, Čubrilović was asked why
he sacrificed his personal family happiness to support Princip's
cause. "I was afraid that a revolutionary organization stood behind
Princip. I saw that behind them stood powerful elements. I [came
to that conclusion] because one doesn't find bombs on the street."[2]
While Princip admitted to having threatened Čubrilović's family
if he spoke about the plot, he was careful to assure the judges that
he "just said that in order to impress him."[3]

Led by Čubrilović along some muddy paths, they came to the
house of an old peasant named Mitar Kerović, the head of a *zadruga*
(collective). Mitar must have felt obliged to offer his assistance
to Čubrilović, not just because he probably sympathized with the
assassination attempt but also because his guest was the godfather of his children. Late at night, a sleepy Princip remembered
the teacher jumping up and excitedly showing the weapons to the
other peasants, including some who had arrived later.[4] Drinking
šljivovica throughout the evening had made him boastful and
imprudent. The peasants had been drinking steadily, too. When
asked by the judge how much he had been drinking, old Mitar
replied, "When I drink, I don't keep count. I drink as much as I
can."[5] Despite the peasants' obvious lack of sophistication (none
of the Kerović clan knew much about the political situation of the
day nor even their own age with certainty), the judges sentenced
Nedjo to be hanged (commuted to life imprisonment) and Mitar to
life imprisonment. As Dedijer notes, "in an Austrian dungeon, old
Mitar and his son Nedjo had to pay with their lives for the secret of
this night."[6]

After a long journey by horse and wagon, the two assassins got
off near Tuzla, washed their clothes in a creek, and bought new
pants (to avoid a travelled appearance, which might have been
noted by people who knew them since they'd gone to high school
there for a year, and also to avoid a vagrancy charge). In the meantime, the peasants who had driven them (Nedjo, who had wanted

to go to Tuzla anyway to have his injured hand examined, and a neighbour, Cvijan Stjepanović), paid a visit to the next contact, a man with a handlebar mustache and a sloping chin called Miško Jovanović. Jovanović was a prominent citizen of Tuzla, the "president of several Serbian clubs, a member of the Eastern Orthodox lay Church Council, and of the Board of Directors of the Serbian Bank, a businessman and owner of the first cinema in Tuzla."[7] Having a wife and a newborn, he had much more to lose than to gain by his involvement in the plot. So when the peasants placed the bombs and pistols on his kitchen table and passed him a letter from Veljko Čubrilović, his best man, this agent of the *Narodna Odbrana* had a moment of doubt.

The two students met Jovanović in the Serbian reading room, which was on the second floor of his house. After moving to a quieter corner, they requested that he transport the weapons to Sarajevo. At the trial, Jovanović denied asking them what the weapons were for, though at the inquiry Danilo Ilić claimed he had discussed the assassination with Jovanović (later he tried to retract the statement). For some reason Grabež incriminated Jovanović by snidely noting that "as an intelligent person he could have figured it out."[8] The investigating judge, Leo Pfeffer, concluded that Jovanović knew about the preparations in advance, and wouldn't have accepted bombs and revolvers in his home from some unknown students, even if they were recommended by his best man. Jovanović refused to transport the weapons but agreed to hold them for a few days until someone came to pick them up. He suggested the person identify himself with a pack of *Stefanija* [*sic*] cigarettes ("because I always smoke *Stefanija* cigarettes"[9]). He also claimed Princip threatened him, "Don't play around with the idea of betraying us, Sir, because I will destroy you and your entire family."[10] In his own defense at the trial, he went on, "Now, gentlemen, I have a wife and a child which she carried for seven months under the heart, and why should my family suffer. Then I thought that those two peasants [who delivered the arms] also had families, and Veljko is my god-relative, and I absolutely could not...prevent it....I had no idea about the conspiracy. They didn't say that they wanted to kill the Heir. Had I known, I would have said, 'Wait, man. Think it over'....I was in a difficult position....I did not have reason to make so many people unhappy."[11]

After seeing Jovanović, Princip and Grabež went to meet Čabrinović, who had arrived in Tuzla two days earlier. The tension was still between them, and they wouldn't tell him where the weapons were ("they didn't trust me"[12]). At the café, Čabrinović further entrenched their opinion of him by getting into a conversation with a detective who said he had seen his father just the day before. He asked Čabrinović where he had been, and Čabrinović said he had been in Dalmatia and Serbia. On the train he spoke with the detective again, but this time managed to be of some use to the conspiracy. The detective obligingly informed him of the date of the archduke's visit to Sarajevo, which they hadn't known before.

When the conspirators arrived in Saraejvo on June 4, it was decided that Danilo Ilić would travel to Tuzla to pick up the weapons.[13] Ilić met Jovanović on June 14, displayed the pack of *Štefanija* cigarettes, and instead of taking the weapons asked Jovanović to deliver them to the railway station in Doboj. The reason for this, he said, was because he was concerned the police in Tuzla might have detained him, being a stranger in town. Jovanović removed the weapons from the cardboard box in the dining room table, packed them in a black sugar box, wrapped it in newspaper, and tied it with string like a parcel. Ilić wasn't there at the appointed hour, forcing Jovanović to leave the box in a waiting room, covered by his coat, and to go in search of him. Was Ilić's personal crisis about the wisdom of assassinating Ferdinand, as well as his icy realization about the serious consequences to himself, another reason for his delay? Whatever the case, he finally showed up, picked up the parcel, and returned to Sarajevo, where he hid the weapons in a suitcase under the bed on which Princip

Electrical plant, Tuzla.

slept. His crisis, as we shall see, only deepened in the coming weeks as he grappled with himself and with Princip over the value of the assassination.

✦ Our trip to Tuzla was uneventful save for a brief encounter with some Muslim women wearing the hijab who were walking on the side of the busy road. When I asked to speak to them, they waved me away, speaking shrilly in a language I didn't understand. After passing industrial outskirts including a chemical factory that spewed yellow smoke from a needle-thin smoke stack, and an electrical power plant that reminded me of Three Mile Island, we arrived in Tuzla. The third largest city in Bosnia after Sarajevo and Banja Luka, with a population of roughly 160,000, Tuzla is a mostly modern city of concrete monoliths in a valley encircled by steep hills. A main avenue pleasantly lined by tall plane and

The view of Tuzla from the Muslim cemetery. Right: Muslim cemetery in Tuzla.

chestnut trees took us into the older part of town, past a university where students in the hundreds walked along. One leggy, beautiful girl after another went past.

"Unbelievable!" my father marvelled. "This is where you come if you want a wife."

Farther on, the wooded avenue led into a shopping district, which reminded me of Zagreb's Ilica Street in the early 1990s when Western capitalism finally began to make inroads. The stores sold familiar commodities by Sony, Chanel, DKNY, and so on, along with no-name stuff reminiscent of the Yugo period—bland polyester shirts, plastic-looking leather jackets, and such—and Turkish items available in other Muslim towns throughout the country like coffee pots, coffee grinders, copper tea sets, Bosnian carpets, and posters of former President Alija Izetbegović, who died in 2003. From such signs you could always tell which of the

two Bosnian federations you were in and what ethnic group was the majority. In Višegrad, a biography of former Bosnian-Serb general and indicted war criminal, Ratko Mladić, was sold at kiosks.

We drove upwards along twisting residential streets until we came to the end of the road where a large Muslim graveyard built at the top of the hill commanded a beautiful view of the valley. From so high up, Tuzla looked as though it had a farmer's tan, divided as it was into a white concrete area and an orange tiled residential one. These sections of the city seemed to narrate Tuzla's evolution from past to present. I got out of the car and climbed to the top through the slick grass between the headstones. From there I could see far to the north, where big hills rolled onward into the clouds.

When I came back down, I noticed a man gazing down at the city. I thought he was admiring the view until I saw him peeing in the grass. He knew we were there but had just turned casually to the side. He was an elderly man; white hair fringed the side of his bald head, and his dark eyebrows gave him the appearance of an owl.

I approached him and started a conversation, eventually getting around to asking him about life in Tuzla these days. "Tuzla is a quiet place now," he said cheerfully, "no problems between the people. I've always been able to get along with anybody, doesn't matter to me."

His easiness about social relations in Tuzla, though, was contradicted by an adamantine memory of what happened here. "The Serbs were up there," he said pointing around at the hills, "and we were down there. You know the story." He looked sternly at me. "My son was hit by a shell. We didn't think he was going to make it. That's not something you forget too soon."

After we'd talked for a while and were about to leave, I asked if I could take a photo of him.

> *Hamdija Ćustendil.*

"Sure," he laughed, "take a picture of me with the Serbian church in the valley!"

His two children came down from the cemetery. Both lived out of the country now, the daughter in Germany, the son in Spain. The daughter didn't like it that I'd taken her father's picture and liked it even less that I asked for his name. "Dad!" she warned him when he was about to tell me. She asked me my name and my reason for coming to Tuzla. I understood her concern, and I understood, too, how she hoped to learn how safe the information would be on the basis of my ethnic background. Her father said, "I don't have anything to fear, I am Hamdija Ćustendil." And he told her to write it in my notebook so I would get it right.

While his daughter seemed to relax, his son never did. Unlike his father, he was embittered about the past and the Serbs who still lived in his city. "You know, I have no reason to deal with them any longer. I hate them now and I will hate them tomorrow." He explained that he'd been injured in the massacre that took place in Tuzla's old town on May 25, 1995. Seventy-one people aged mostly between eighteen and twenty-five died from a bomb fired from Serbian positions on Mount Ozren.[14] This terrible attack occurred on May 25, which was once the officially celebrated birthday of former Yugoslav president Tito. That it happened at all proved the extraordinary inadequacy of the UN-mandated safe-havens throughout Bosnia-Herzegovina.

Hamdija's son's hatred for the Serbs was deeply personal, but his cynical (though reserved) attitude about the Croats had a less obvious origin. Although he seemed to consider us "better" on his scale of things, at least during our brief encounter, he didn't love us either. This became obvious when he laughed after I'd told him I'd written a travel book about Croatia.

"Very good!' he sneered. "You should write about Croatia-in-Bosnia." This was a reference to the irredentist aims of the

> *Turalibeg Mosque, Tuzla.*

Tudjman regime in Croatia proper during the 1990s as well as a hint about the fiercely xenophobic Croats in Herzegovina. In his mind, they were no better than the Serbs who sought a greater Serbia at the expense of the Muslims.

I could sense my father getting restless as he listened to Hamdija's son.

Time to go, I thought. I asked the latter for his first name, which he declined to give me. I offered to take his picture, so that I would have a face to match his words should I ever write about our conversation, but he just shook his head, made a bitter face and said, "Naaaahh."

So we left them (the old man waving cheerily goodbye) and took a last turn through the older section of Tuzla. The rain had held off, the air was calm, and people were out and about. In the narrow, cobbled alleys and side streets, where broken cars sat on concrete blocks and big dogs barked viciously from behind walls, we came across one mosque after another. The recorded wail from a muezzin echoed loudly over the valley. This had long been a mainly Muslim town, I realized, and the Serbs long the minority. For a moment I could imagine how the feeling of being outnumbered manifested itself in paranoia among Serbs throughout Bosnia even before the war in the 1990s. The Serbs in Tuzla could go further back in history to cite actual examples of the real dangers of their situation; after the assassination in 1914, for example, the Austrians herded thousands of Serbs into internment camps in Tuzla and elsewhere.

Now, as we were about to leave, I thought of other regions in the country where the demographics were different but where the story was much the same. While the Serbs of Tuzla had tried to redress the imbalance of power, farther south in Herzegovina the Croats were the ones who had sought to carve out ethnically pure areas. Only the Muslims in Bosnia seemed loyal to the idea of Yugoslavia—like the assassins of 1914—while everyone else wanted to destroy it.

6 ✦ HERZEGOVINA

✦ TEMPERATE CLIMATE/EXTREMIST TEMPERAMENT

ANYONE WHO HAS TRAVELLED through Herzegovina, especially in the summer when the sun hammers down on the arid,
bone-coloured, karst hills, knows the region has a different character than Bosnia to the north. Located in the southeastern part
of the country, Herzegovina has the rugged look of Dalmatia, the
same cruel enmity toward living things, alleviated only by narrow
green bands along rivers like the Neretva, Trebižat, and Bregava.
The people of Herzegovina also differ in some respects from those
in Bosnia; many embrace their regional identity and their ethnic
"nation" (or *narod*) over that of Bosnia-Herzegovina itself.

I visited the capital of Herzegovina, Mostar, in June 2005. The
road south from Sarajevo paralleled the green Neretva as it wound
between imposing mountainous hills covered by forests, through
steep gorges, and past Jablaničko Lake, where a fretwork of

fishing frames and nets hugged the shore. On the way, there were patches of gravel on sharp curves where locals had set up tables to sell honey. It was Sunday, and people walked beside the road on their way to market or to church. As in other parts of the country, there were no stores or other businesses here, the settlements little more than a few houses strung narrowly along the road.

Farther on, though, I came across some log road houses with enormous barbecues out front in which sheep were turning on spits. I was hungry and decided to stop. At this new, impeccable restaurant, the service was fast and the mutton portioned out generously. Even the washroom was grand, with granite countertops and marble tiles. The Croatian owner hadn't spared any expense. The washroom turned out to be more impressive visually than it was functional because once I stepped inside I had to watch my footing on the tiles, which were slick with urine. I was forced to dry off my shoes by walking around the dusty gravel parking lot before getting into the car and driving on to Mostar.

✦ In 1999, when I visited Mostar last, the Muslim sector still showed signs of the heavy beating it had taken from the Croats. Many buildings were gutted, roofless shells like giant rib cages of colossal carcasses. The "old bridge" (*stari most*) from which Mostar got its name lay in pieces on the riverbank, destroyed by Croatian forces on November 9, 1993 (the anniversary of both Kristallnacht and the collapse of the Berlin Wall).

The bridge had stood for 427 years. The Ottoman architect who built it in 1566, Mimar Hajrudin, was convinced it would fall. As one historian explains, "The first span collapsed, and the Sultan, furious, sent for the architect and warned him that, if the next one did not hold, Hajrudin would pay with his head. When at last the bridge was finished the architect was nowhere to be found; certain that it would not stand, he had fled to Bijelo Polje. The

>*The new bridge in Mostar.*

townspeople sought him out and bore him to the Sultan, by whom he was duly congratulated."[1]

For centuries Hajrudin's work had served the people of Mostar in their daily business. In Princip's time, one visitor recalls,

caravans of horses, mules, and donkeys, laden with produce, and herds of sheep and cattle rendered the passage across somewhat risky, and once I was nearly jostled over the low parapet and into the torrent below. And what a babel of tongues! Turkish, Greek, Serb, Albanian, and Croatian— even a species of Lingua-Franca *which passes for Italian on the Dalmatian coast. The costumes would have supplied material for a dozen brilliant ballets—ranging from the seedy frockcoat and fez of the modernised Turk to the real thing from Albania—the swarthy, stalwart savage in gaudy rags, with bright knives and firearms. Occasionally the black cowl of a Moslem woman would flit hurriedly by, as if to escape observation, but no shyness appeared to trouble the Christian fair sex, easily distinguished by their gowns of white cloth and black embroidery, heavy silver ornaments, and flower-bedecked hair.*[2]

When I visited Mostar in 2005, a new bridge spanned the Neretva. But the activity on the bridge wasn't as colourful nor as telling about local life as it used to be. There were middle-aged women in long blouses that hung almost down to their hem lines, big vinyl purses slung over their shoulders; bleach-blonde girls in tight jeans, fat sunglasses, and bright Crocs; and tourists leaning on the parapet to take in the view of the slowly moving river. On one bank was a small pebble beach where some teenagers had gathered and where two guys on mopeds leaned toward each other in quiet conversation and where, farther on, oblivious to the activity near him, an elderly man in a white undershirt hung a fishing line out into the sluggish current. He could have been, I thought, the very man I met in 1999, here still, unflaggingly patient.

When I stepped onto the bridge I saw a young man in a black Speedo, poised to leap into the Neretva, twenty metres below. By

Above and page 114: Diver in Mostar.

the time I got close, he had flung himself outward, and I had just enough time to focus the shot before he hit the water. When he climbed onto the beach he chatted with the kids for a few minutes before returning to the bridge. As I got ready to snap another picture, he stopped me. "The tradition here is that you pay."

I reached into my pocket and fished out a Bosnian mark. He waved it away contemptuously and replied, "Twenty euros for a picture."

So much foreign money had been pumped into Mostar, including financing for projects like the bridge we stood on, that he could be forgiven, I supposed, for expecting more. I wondered why he didn't demand payment from the other tourists waiting to take a shot. I shook my head and left him to make his last preparations. A split second before he jumped I snapped a photo.

It was, I thought, a good time to go. After leaving the bridge, I walked back through the cobble-stoned Turkish Quarter where I was soon surrounded by tourists milling outside shops. Here one could buy the usual copper pots, Turkish rugs, and paintings of the bridge, but you could also find pepper grinders welded out of old shells, currency from the former Yugoslavia, pins from the Yugoslav army, and T-shirts silkscreened with Tito's image. On a side street a man sold pirated CDs on the hood of his beat-up Škoda.

At the Koski Mehmed Paša Mosque, the guide took a German couple and me on a tour. A tall man with black hair and a little mustache like a black smudge on his lip, our guide spoke autocratically in staccato bursts of German, spraying the air from time to time and sewing up each carefully memorized sentence neatly with his fingertips. He told the German husband and me that we were permitted inside the mosque provided we stayed within the roped-off area. The raised wooden platform on the right was designated for women. Our guide pointed out the golden brown inscriptions on the walls. He said one read, "A single truth is worth seventy years of prayer."

After we had wound our way up the coiling stairs of the minaret and seen the spectacular view of the orange roofs of Mostar, our guide led us to the Turkish house where the Muslim *hoða* lived. Part of this house had been converted into a museum, and it was into this that we entered after removing our shoes. The main room of the house had a long couch running along the walls, carpets on the floor, a large ornate serving tray with Turkish coffee cups on a low table, and tall windows shaped at the top like turbans. Through these I could see the Neretva and some houses on the far bank.

"This was the *hoða*'s main room," we were told. "He had four wives. Two skinny ones for the summer and two fat ones for the

winter." The German wife giggled. Our guide almost smiled when he delivered this piece of information, but he managed to stay serious and speak even more autocratically than before.

Before we parted ways, the German wife asked him what life was like in Mostar now. Like other Bosnians to whom I'd put this question, he said relations between ordinary people were always good and still are. "I'm a Muslim, my wife is a Croat. We have three children. She helps here selling items to visitors, and I go to Međugorje [the Catholic pilgrimage site] to help her."

But in private he painted a different picture. Once the Germans had left, he whispered to me in the street, looking left and right as people went by. He had lost his affected speech and hand gestures of earlier. "I tell visitors such things so they leave with a good impression of Bosnia-Herzegovina. But really relations between people here are not so good. How can they be good, I ask you? Everyone lost someone in the war, and they know which side did it. It would be better if we could live as we did in Yugoslavia. But it will take many years before life returns to what it was."

In the garden of the mosque, the Muslim caretaker joined us for a talk about Bosnian history. When I asked him what sprung to mind when he thought of Gavrilo Princip, he reflected for a second then answered categorically, "Bin Laden!"

✦ At the turn of the twentieth century, Mostar was an important intellectual centre in Bosnia-Herzegovina. A new generation of boys of peasant stock born in towns had begun to make inroads into the well-to-do intelligentsia of the time. Unlike the latter, who were politically conservative, satisfied with government posts, and disinclined to rock the Austro-Hungarian boat, the new generation was far more radical. Many promising but disadvantaged Serbian and Bosnian-Serb students received scholarships from the Serbian government to study in Vienna, Prague, Zagreb,

< Turkish house where the hoda lived, Mostar.

and Belgrade, where they were first introduced to revolutionary political doctrines, as well as modern intellectual thought and society. Their new ways of thinking ran aground, however, when they returned to their villages, where the peasants, conservative by nature, were held back even more by the policies of the Austro-Hungarian regime, which entrenched tribalism and feudalism. Moreover, the authorities banned free political discussions and societies. Mostar's high school was thus one of the "intellectual cradles of the Young Bosnians."[3]

Tensions between students in Mostar and the Austrian authorities were at a high pitch just a few months before the assassination when the students went on strike. Noted Serbian-American physicist Michael Pupin blamed Austria's policy of repression for the strike and the assassination. Commenting on the evening of June 28, 1914, he said:

> The student strike began, you remember, when a Government professor in the school of Mostar, Herzegovina, made violent attacks on the Serb race. The students of his class rose in a body and asked him to retract. He refused. They pitched him out of the class room and used him rather roughly. These fifty students went on strike. They are only high school students really, boys about 16 to 19 years old. But their patriotism is inflammable. They refused to return until the professor was dismissed. They were expelled. Then throughout Herzegovina and Bosnia the students struck in sympathy. The Government sent troops and officers to restore order. The students refused to give in. And so the fight stands deadlocked.[4]

Mostar was also the site of a meeting in May 1914 between Danilo Ilić and Mehmed Mehmedbašić, a Muslim carpenter from Stolac who agreed to participate in the assassination attempt. Mehmedbašić had long had a taste for assassination, if not the stomach for it. In January 1914, he liberated the last two peasants owned by his father, a feudal lord, and with the money financed his trip to Toulouse, where he had a meeting with expatriate

Bosnian-Serb revolutionary and Black Hand member Vladimir Gaćinović, as well as some other Young Bosnians. It was decided that Mehmedbašić would carry out an assassination of then Bosnian governor Oskar Potiorek who had enforced the so-called "exceptional measures" against rebellious South Slavs in Bosnia. Mehmedbašić told historian Luigi Albertini the following story:

> A dagger was chosen as the surest weapon, especially if poisoned before-hand. Gaćinović gave me a little bottle of poison with which I was to moisten the blade of the dagger before doing the deed. From Toulouse I went to Marseilles and there embarked for Ragusa [Dubrovnik]. At Ragusa I took the train, but I noticed that gendarmes were searching the compartments for something. Fearing I was the man they wanted I threw away the dagger and poison in the lavatory. I afterward found that it was a petty thief they were after. When I reached Stolac I wrote Gaćinović and, pending his reply, did nothing more about carrying out the outrage.[5]

The route by which Mehmedbašić became one of the assassins on June 28 wasn't clearly explained by Ilić, who contradicted his earlier statements at the investigation when at the trial he said Mehmedbašić had given him the idea for the assassination before Princip did.[6] In any case, the example of a radical Bosnian Muslim acting side by side with Bosnian Serbs served the purpose of suggesting that the assassination had support across Bosnia (which was not entirely incorrect). With the arrival of the Austrians, a small number of the Muslim elite called themselves "Serbs of the Muslim faith" or "Muslim Serbs," which was "primarily a reflection of their political attraction to the independent, vigorously nationalistic, and expansionist Serbian state as a potential counterweight to Austrian power."[7] But Mehmedbašić's involvement was certainly more the exception than the rule; the Austrian period also saw the expansion of separate Muslim religious, cultural, educational, economic, and political organizations. The word "Muslim" changed from a narrow religious term into a broader ethnic, national identity, to distinguish Bosnian Muslims from Serbs and Croats.[8] Since the last war, the term "Muslim" has been replaced by "Bosniak," and the language they speak changed in official and unofficial parlance from "Serbo-Croatian" to "Bosnian," for similar purposes. These changes irritate some Croats and Serbs, many of whom go back five and a half centuries in order to say that Bosnia's Muslims aren't really Muslims at all, but originally ethnic Croats or Serbs who converted to Islam during the Ottoman period.

✦ After a day of rest on the Croatian coast, I returned to Herzegovina via the border crossing near Crveni Grm. It was already stiflingly hot at nine in the morning as I climbed waves of limestone-pocked spurs, leaving the vineyards of Dalmatia's hinterland behind. At the border I chatted with the Croatian officer, a paunchy, flaccid-faced man who wore aviator sunglasses and a big smile that bared his yellow horse teeth. On taking my passport and seeing my name, he didn't bother recording my car registration and car rental agreement number, which had been the norm at other crossings controlled by Muslims and Serbs.

I asked him if the next town, Ljubuški, was a "Croatian town." What I meant to ask was whether Ljubuški was populated mainly by Croats. He laughed at that and shook his head and said ruefully, "It ought to be, but unfortunately it's just Bosnia-Herzegovina."

He wished me good luck, and I drove into the valley on the Herzegovinan side of the mountains. I saw more flat lands covered by vast vineyards, large houses with well-tended gardens, courtyards covered by grapevines, and fruit stands, where watermelons sat in buckets cooled by running sprinklers. The hot, dry wind blowing through the car's open windows carried the electrical sound of crickets. At Ljubuški—a lively, fair-sized town, home to many new businesses, houses, and Catholic churches—I turned north and drove in the direction of Livno. Beside the plethora of large gardens and vineyards, I saw an abandoned mosque and a Muslim graveyard overgrown by quack grass.

The clerk at a post office assured me that there were plenty of Muslims about, and some were still her friends. She had only good things to say about them. When I mentioned how nice Herzegovina was, she wasn't as enthusiastic. "You think?" was her reaction.

In Studenci I stopped for a break at a large Catholic church a few hundred metres off the road. Enormous pine trees in the parking area offered the only shade, and when I stepped out of the car, the heat hit me hard, settling heavily on me like a weight. There was no wind, no life, only the sawing sound of crickets from the rocky hills. I descended some steps and walked toward a line of stunted, dusty trees that snaked through a field. When I got there I noticed some dense grass on the banks of a little stream, which moved so languidly it hardly seemed to move at all. At my noisy arrival dozens of tiny frogs leaped into the stream and yellow butterflies, startled by the commotion, fluttered around for half a minute before settling on the grass. Through the trees, which leaned across the water, shafts of sunlight touched the dark surface, flickering off the wings of metallic-blue dragonflies. This was a quiet place, one of those watery oases in the hard, dry Herzegovinan countryside. I sat there for half an hour, out of the heat, until I finally wrenched myself away and headed back to the car.

After this short break by the stream, I headed east, stopping in Čapljina. The city was hot, silent, and dead. At midday no one was outside save for some apparently unemployed people at the main street's abundant cafés. In Studenci the stream had spared me for a while from the heat, but in Čapljina the afternoon sun glinting off the socialist block apartments was suffocating, and every café was like an oasis.

In a clothing boutique, one of the few stores open for some reason, a saleswoman I met felt that her life had been suffocated, too. This wasn't just because the economy had gone to hell but also because she hated the new Bosnia-Herzegovina. Her nation was Croatia.

"When Croatia plays football, I watch the game. When Bosnia plays I couldn't care less."

Her large green eyes made her tanned face almost attractive, if you could get beyond the hint of skull under her tight skin. She talked freely to me after I introduced myself, my use of the word *kaj* ("what" in northern parts of Croatia) a signal that I was okay.

"Look," she went on, "I'm not interested much in politics, but I can tell you that my grandad was *Ustaša*, my dad was *Ustaša*, and I'm *Ustaša*. We need an *Ustaša* army now, isn't that right?" She smiled, a pretty smile, trying to draw me in. The *Ustaše* were Croatian fascists in the Second World War who slaughtered opponents of their regime (mainly Serbs). As one western Herzegovinan said about his region, "Only three things grow here: snakes, stones and Ustashas."[9]

This form of ethno-nationalistic extremism resulted in some of the worst fighting in the most recent war. Around Mostar, the conflict eventually pitted Croats against Muslims. Many Croats in Herzegovina wanted to ethnically cleanse the region and either establish a mini state (like the Serbs in the Krajina) or ultimately join Croatia itself.

"To be honest I can tolerate the Serbs more than these Muslims. Of course I have Muslim friends, I'm not speaking of them, but Muslims in general. They simply repulse me. I can never be sure they are clean. Like animals. And then they shake your hand. That to me is disgusting!"

She spoke with the sort of unrestrained conviction, the absence of doubt, I'd encountered before in the former Yugoslavia, but when I asked her her name or permission to take a photo, she refused. Like Hamdija's son in Tuzla, she wasn't willing to put a face to her words.

✦ I left her and headed toward the town of Stolac. Since I was so close, I decided to visit Radmilja, the site of a necropolis of an Orthodox Vlach family called Miloradović. The tombstones there, or *stećci*, have become well-known as apparent examples of Bogomil handiwork, and while they weren't related to the story I was exploring, they seemed attuned to its darker spirit and my mood at the time. Dating from between the fourteenth to sixteenth centuries, the *stećci* lie unceremoniously off a narrow road leading into Stolac, in a meadow surrounded by tall cypresses. Some Gypsy kids were running through the graveyard and jumping off the stones. As I walked through the necropolis, they ran off and watched me shyly from a distance. The *stećci* I saw were sizable stone blocks, many upright and engraved with bas-reliefs depicting warriors with their arms raised in greeting, bow and arrow over their left shoulders. After all this time the stones were weather-stained and leaned from the stresses of the earth. Still, their size and number were impressive, giving me a sense of the wealth and power of the clan that had many of them built.

Scholars have questioned the assumption still prevalent in Bosnia-Herzegovina that such stones were Bogomil in origin. American historian John Fine says they have been called Bogomil because of the belief that the Bosnian Church, a heretical Catholic offshoot unique to Bosnia, was Bogomil, and "the further belief that since these stones seem to have been idiosyncratic to Bosnia and since the Bosnians have their own local church, the stones must be related to that Church."[10] But such stones aren't evident in Bosnia alone, where the Church was active. Also, their inscriptions suggest they were erected by wealthy people of all faiths.

As I stood among the *stećci*, I had one of those unsettling moments that came to me often on my travels in the former Yugoslavia—a sense of deep time in relation to which I seemed to grow small in importance. But more than that, the *stećci* of Radmilja were imparting a lesson to everyone, including the

assassins in 1914: the very most we can aspire to, despite our vanities, ambitions, and self-importance, is the silent presence of tombstones in a graveyard that is a playground for Gypsy children.

✦ After the necropolis, I made the decision to take another break from my journey and travel to Bosnia's "riviera" on the Adriatic Sea. I wanted to leave the assassins behind for a while, as well as the emotional heaviness of "that" Bosnia. Rather than complicate matters by crossing into Croatia at Metković, I turned inland at Dračevo, on the road toward Neum. On the map the trip looked simple enough. And at first it was, as the road took me along the flat, marshy area around the Hutovo Bird Sanctuary, but then it led me up into the first range of enormous hills that rolled wave after wave to the south. Up I went on the first of many switchbacks, cut like long incisions on the side of the hills, higher and higher above the sanctuary, until the lake appeared below me like a patch of blue seen from a plane. In the beginning the road was good, but narrow, and it nearly threw me into a gorge to make room for a white van that sped around a corner.

Once I crested the first range I finally made some headway south. But it was slow going over a worsening road that wound wickedly around ever more hills. Between the climbs and descents were short, flat stretches where a house or two sat orphaned and an old man leaned against the brick wall of his shack, staring emptily at my car, and a bony goat grazed on a patch of dry grass. From the rocky land grew tough, gnarly bushes, a few willows, and some olive trees. The latter encouraged me because they told me I was nearing the coast. After nearly an hour, when I thought I saw the blue of the ocean, I was disappointed to find it was only the sky hanging above more of the same endlessly rolling hills. Was there no end to them? Had I taken the right road? Maybe this one led east into Montenegro instead of south to Neum. This was

< Radmilja necropolis, near Stolac.

exactly the sort of unpopulated place my cousin, the anaesthesiologist in Croatia, had warned me about. *You can just disappear.* There was nothing I could do but swear at myself and keep driving. This wasn't the first time I'd taken a godforsaken road in Bosnia by mistake, but I told myself it would be the last. I gripped the wheel tight, concentrated on avoiding broken sections of asphalt and keeping the car on the road.

Not long after, I saw the Croatian flag with its checkerboard *šahovnica* hanging from an electrical wire. This, for me, was a comforting sight. Then a car appeared at high speed, its driver waving cheerfully as he went past. He probably waved to everyone, just as people did in rural Nova Scotia where I spent my summers. This area was as safe a place for him as Antigonish county was to me. You're a fool, I told myself, as I made the last descent to the border crossing, from where I could see the Adriatic glittering in the distance.

✦ Despite the promise to myself, I was forced to drive yet another road comparable to this one the following summer. After our visit to Foča, my father and I headed to Trebinje in southeastern Herzegovina on the last leg of our trip through eastern Republika Srpska. By the time we left Foča, the late afternoon sun had begun to slip behind the forested hills.

It wasn't long before we entered a truly mountainous region. Here, the Dinaric Alps rise up and rumble into Montenegro, which lies just a few kilometres to the east. In Sutjeska National Park, the last of the houses fell away and deep, silent forests crowded the road, and a large meadow appeared with two enormous monuments. Built by the Yugoslav communists in commemoration of a Tito-led Partisan victory over a massive Axis force during the Second World War, the monuments stood on the crest of a hill against a backdrop of thick evergreens. One of the structures looked like great shards of rock that had been welded together as they plummeted through the atmosphere and impaled the earth.

Monument commemorating the Battle of Sutjeska during the Second World War.

Their design was impressive, and their position above the road had been carefully considered to produce the most powerful aesthetic and emotional effect.

I got out of the car. It had rained recently, but the sun had come out and was shining on the flower-sprinkled meadow. The valley was silent and peaceful. I noticed a path leading through the grass to the monuments, so I asked my father if he wanted to get a closer look.

He was still inside the car, with his glasses off, squinting at the map. "What for?" he answered without looking up.

"It might be worth seeing."

"Forget it. Drive on," he said.

"Are you sure? I might get a good picture."

"You can take one from here. Let's go."

Ever since his escape from Yugoslavia in 1964, and probably before then, he had disliked Tito's regime and all its self-congratulatory propaganda. In this way, he was no different than most Croats today. But Tito's achievement as leader of the Partisans during the Second World War, and this battle in particular, which was in some historians' opinion a turning point in the Balkan campaign, was held in high esteem by many Yugoslavs. The enormous sacrifice on the part of the Partisans, which included numerous Serbs, was trumpeted throughout twentieth-century Yugoslav history and was a point of thematic connection with the young South Slavic nationalists of 1914, who martyred themselves on behalf of their people. This self-sacrifice shouldn't be summarily dismissed. But one can't help wondering whether the latest story the Serbs told themselves and the world during the most recent war, a story about persecution and sacrifice, was a less honourable one.

My father was right about not visiting the monuments; it was getting late, and we had a long road ahead of us before we reached Trebinje, which as far as we knew was the only place where we could spend the night. I decided to drive on.

It wasn't long before we entered the savage jaws of the Alps, passing through deep gorges, under cliffs hanging precariously over the road, and beside white water raging in loud muscular torrents below. On all sides, grey serrated crags tore low clouds into ribbons and flung the road viciously back and forth. Up it climbed into the clouds, leading us in steep hairpins toward the summit. From there the forested valleys were wrapped in the pall of rain-heavy clouds and coming evening. I saw a snowy mountaintop appear for a moment, float on a white feathery bed, then disappear.

We were all alone. Even the road didn't want to be here, collapsing totally in places or sliding in great slabs down the side of the mountain. As we crested the final peak, at the point when I thought we were home free, the gas light came on, and the car's computer screen said we had thirty-five kilometres left in the tank.

We descended through wide open, rocky terrain that rolled in easy waves toward the coast, disappearing into purple darkness at the far edges as dusk settled over the land. There were no cars, no houses, no people. The screen read twenty kilometres.

"What do we do now?" I asked my father.

"Nothing, just keep driving."

"How much farther until Gačko?" Gačko was a large town where there was sure to be a gas station.

He took off his glasses, crunched up his eyebrows and squinted at the map again. "Let's see. Uuhhh...around thirty-seven kilometres."

"Whadya mean thirty-seven kilometres?" I said. "You said forty half an hour ago."

"I guess we didn't go very far."

"Maybe if you put your glasses on when you look at that map you would get it right," I said angrily. "What are we going to do? It's getting dark."

"I guess you'll be sleeping in the car, sonny boy!" he laughed.

I wished I had listened to my instincts when we'd passed a gas station a few hours ago. I kept driving, lifting my foot off the gas whenever we went downhill. I hoped we would see a house or a hamlet, but not a soul lived in this part of Herzegovina. As I looked out at the indistinct contours of the rocky emptiness that was quickly fading to dark, I thought I heard the engine sputter a few times. I resigned myself to a night in our car.

Finally, to my relief, the road descended toward a big plain where the lights of a sprawling settlement twinkled in the grow-ing dark. We passed a small fair with a lit up Ferris wheel and bumper cars. It was a crazy sight, a slice of rural America trans-planted to the Herzegovinan wilderness. In the dusk the rest of Gačko looked American, too, but in a different way, like a desert town in Texas or Arizona.

We were happy to have arrived. The gas attendant waved his hand to the south and said we had less than an hour's drive to Trebinje. It was a good road, he said. Just stay on it. And so we drove on in the dark until we reached the city.

Finding a place to sleep in Trebinje turned out to be easier than I thought; no sooner had we parked in front of a pair of motels than the owner of one spotted us, sprinted out and asked if we needed a room. Anyone that vigilant deserved our business, so we drove into the back and parked. Once we got our bags out of the trunk, the security guard (I use the term loosely because he was the twenty-year-old nephew of the owner), pulled up the steel post behind the car and locked it into place. Thieves had been known to steal vehicles and drive them into Montenegro. But nothing about Bosnia fazed us anymore; we gave up our passports, ate a meal, and went to sleep.

✦ After a rain shower during the night, the morning dawned fresh and clean. A pale sun shone behind a thin film of clouds as we stepped out into the newer section of Trebinje. Through the mainly empty streets a few people were taking their Sunday constitutional. Among them was an elderly Serb on his way home. He wore a grey suit, a white shirt open at the collar, and a brown felt cap. He spoke in the same upright and tidy manner as he dressed.

It didn't seem the right moment to begin another heavy discussion about war and ethnicity, though I'm sure he wouldn't have been perturbed by the subject, nor liable to start a diatribe as I might have expected from someone else. He was a steady, civil man, a retired lawyer as it turned out.

Because Trebinje was so far from the centre of Bosnia-Herzegovina, and on the margins of the country, a stone's throw from Montenegro, I asked him how he defined himself.

> *Retired lawyer in Trebinje.*

"If you are asking whether I think of myself as a Bosnian, I will tell you that I do not. Or perhaps it is better to say that I am not Bosnian *first*. I am a Herzegovinan. I was born in Herzegovina and lived most of my life in Herzegovina. The region comes first before anything else."

"But you are a Serb. Does Herzegovina come before being a Serb?" I asked.

"Yes, Herzegovina comes first."

I mentioned my encounter with the Croat shopkeeper in Čapljina. "Do the Serbs here look to Serbia the way the Croats in Herzegovina turn to Croatia?"

"Of course. Whoever you are you can't escape such ties, nor should you try. But Serbs in Trebinje think of themselves as Herzegovinan first."

Such thinking ran counter to the intense ethnocentric irredentism I'd encountered so far in the region.

"Our identities here are layered," he went on, "and these layers are not always the same in every person. Even the town where you live, and the streets you walk, shape you in important ways."

"But at the end of the day, being a Serb takes precedent over coming from Trebinje," I said.

"Sadly it does, for some."

We looked at each other and nodded. "Will it always be like this? " I wondered.

He just shrugged and threw up his hands. On that note he wished me luck on the rest of my travels and said goodbye.

As we were driving to the old town, my father said, "I don't think people will ever be different. You can talk as much as you want about higher values and living like brothers. But I tell you this: if the UN leaves Bosnia there's going to be trouble again. Maybe not right away, but sooner or later they'll be at each other's throats."

"Maybe."

"You better believe it."

The pleasant morning was discouraging such thoughts. The pale sun of earlier now shone strongly through gossamer clouds and onto the wet streets, releasing here and there a mist from the flagstones. Old Trebinje had the look of a Dalmatian town, with its cream-coloured stone buildings, wooden shutters, and smoothly polished *corso* or promenade. Trees shaded people from the sun and round lamps lined up along the centre of the promenade hung in the warm fragrant morning like full moons. As I walked around Trebinje, taking in its understated Mediterranean atmosphere, I realized that it showed few signs of damage from the war. Maybe this was because the Serbs had had little trouble driving out its Muslim neighbours and had therefore spared most of the town a protracted conflict.[11]

We strolled through the quiet streets for a while until we came to a small, newly built mosque, the only sign of a Muslim presence I'd seen. A man was leaning against a garden wall smoking, and my father asked him when the building was constructed.

"I know nothing about Muslims," was his abrupt answer.

My father informed him that I was a travel writer working on a book about Bosnia. Suddenly the guy grew friendlier. He said he could help me and tell me the truth about his country. After leading us to a nearby café, and paying for our drinks, he told us he was born in a village near Ljubuški but had been living in Trebinje since 1993. A bricklayer by trade, he did odd jobs now to support his three kids. He didn't mention a wife.

His booming voice filled the café. "I'm not against anybody," he shouted. "I've lived with everyone, Serb or Croat or Muslim, it doesn't matter. A few years ago there was a demonstration against the Muslims coming back, but I wasn't part of it. What the fuck would I achieve by doing that, let me ask you? Nothing, that's what, so I steered clear of the whole thing. Listen, I know how those people feel 'cause I was in the same boat. I had a house in Ljubuški, a decent place, nothing special, and when the war started the Croats sent me packing. What the hell was I gonna

do?" His right hand landed heavily on the table. "But I'm not pissed off about it. I live here now, and that life is history."

He lit another cigarette. After a pause he said, "I know the guy who destroyed my house, burned it to the ground. We went to school together. You know the deal. A couple years ago I went back to see him. He wasn't hard to find. He lived down the street."

"What did you do" I asked.

"I didn't do anything. I shook his hand. I went there and shook his hand. He invited me for a *rakija* and we spent the afternoon on his veranda talking."

His fist pounded the table. "Come on, we'll go there now. I can introduce you to him. He can tell you why he burned down my house."

My father laughed.

The bricklayer laughed, too, then leaning forward and tapping my father's arm with the outside of his left hand, said, "You understand what I'm telling you, sir, it's a crazy situation but it's normal, it's fucking normal."

"What else can you do?" my father said.

"That's it. And you know what else, I want to say this, this is important," he added, pointing at me, "pay attention now, there comes a point when the road we've been on has to end, when we have to stop hating."

"You could have taken matters into your own hands," I said.

He shrugged. "So it will never end."

Up to now he'd been talking in his loud, unrestrained voice so that the only other person in the café, the waitress, could hear every word. But suddenly he leaned forward and began to whisper.

"My father was a Serb, but my mother was a Croat. I guess you could say I'm a bit of mixed bag like one of those mutts you see on the street and think to yourself, hey there's some German shepherd and some fox terrier and maybe some wolf in that package.

< Author's father and man in Trebinje.

But you really don't know. The point is this, there's plenty more like me in this country, everywhere you look, everywhere you go. And you have to make choices, or maybe it's better to say choices are made for you."

Through the thick smoke I saw him spread his big arms wide and say, loud and indiscrete again, "I AM BOSNIA."

He smiled, and we smiled, and then he began to talk about other matters like the future of his teenaged son, the economy in Trebinje, and so on. He asked what it was like in Canada and whether jobs were readily available. When we left the café he shook our hands energetically and told us we would always be welcome in his home, just look him up. Then he posed for a photograph.

БЛАГО ТОМЕ КО ДОВИЈЕК ЖИВИ ИМАО СЕ РАШТА И РОДИТИ

ВИДОВДАНСКИ ХЕРОЈИ

ГАВРИЛО ПРИНЦИП
НЕДЕЉКО ЧАБРИНОВИЋ   ДАНИЛО ИЛИЋ   ТРИФКО ГРАБЕЖ
ВЕЉКО ЧУБРИЛОВИЋ   МИХАЈЛО МИШКО ЈОВАНОВИЋ   МИТАР КЕРОВИЋ
НЕЂО КЕРОВИЋ   ЈАКОВ МИЛОВИЋ   МАРКО ПЕРИН
БОГДАН ЖЕРАЈИЋ

1914

✦ VIDOVDAN, 1914

EVERY TIME I REMEMBER travelling from Tuzla to Sarajevo in the spring of 2006, I think of the guy who told me to "sucka my dick." It was the only incident on a quiet trip, which paralleled the one long ago of the three assassins and their organizer, Danilo Ilić. My father and I passed through more of the same rolling country of plum trees typical of northern Bosnia, shabby roadside stores, brick houses, and mangy chained dogs staring listlessly at the traffic. Near Sarajevo, where the terrain becomes hillier, the only occasion to stop for us turned out to be a small grocery store that sold hard liquor. Even though my father had trouble reading a map a few inches from his nose, he could see a mickey in a shop window at a hundred paces while sitting in a car travelling eighty kilometres an hour at dusk.

Not reacting quickly to his order to stop, I missed the entrance and had to turn around and come back. When I entered the parking lot, I heard shouts from a group of young guys sitting on a pile of used tires. As my father got out and went into the store, the shouts continued, and eventually a tall, skinny, blonde guy around twenty-five years old approached the car. He kept pointing angrily at another entrance farther down the road, which was by the neighbouring gas station. As he went on barking at me, I ignored him and kept looking ahead. This turned out to be the wrong thing to do.

Before I knew it he had opened my door.

"You took the wrong fucking entrance!! See over there, that's the one you have to use. You can't enter through the exit. Can't you read the signs?" He was leaning down, his head a few inches from my face.

"What?" I asked in English. "I don't speak Bosnian. *No speakati Bosnian.*"

It took a moment for his mind to grapple with this information. Then he switched to English.

"You take wrong road. You must not take wrong road. See over there, that is road you must drive. There is law in Bosnia, and you break law in Bosnia."

I threw up my hands.

He slammed the door in disgust and went back to his buddies.

When my father returned and we were about to leave, he rolled down the window and asked the blonde guy what his problem was. "Why does it bother you whether we drive here or there?"

Stupidly, and more lamely than before, he went through his reasons all over again. His friends were quiet, but they were grinning in a dirty way, enjoying the spectacle.

"Forget it," I told my father. "The guy's drunk."

And yet I didn't listen to my own advice, waving goodbye with my middle finger.

As I drove off, our Bosnian friend grabbed his crotch and yelled, "Sucka my dick, sucka my dick!"

There are idiots wherever you travel, not only in Bosnia, and this was probably just an isolated incident. But I wondered whether this particular idiot was telling me something about his life, without really meaning to. How many others were there like him, living in a country still recovering from a war, guys with no jobs and nothing better to do than drink and harass people on the side of the road on a Friday night?

✦ We arrived in Sarajevo half an hour later and took a room at the Hotel Saraj, which was situated on top of a hill near the old town, and which had been rebuilt after taking multiple hits from the Bosnian Serbs. In the morning we went into the city.

On June 4, 1914, the conspirators also arrived in Sarajevo. Then they dispersed—Grabež to his family in Pale, Čabrinović to his father's home in Sarajevo, and Princip first to his brother's in Hadžići and then to Stoja Ilić's house on Oprkanj Street. Čabrinović had been wary of returning home, expecting more trouble with his parents, especially with his father. To his surprise, however, he found them friendly and inviting. At the trial he recalled, "When I came home it was very pleasant for me, they welcomed me, which I had not expected. I felt very comfortable that they welcomed me in such a way. Later I was reconciled and felt good. Then when I asked Princip, 'How goes it?' he waved his hand. I was completely reconciled to the situation."[1]

During the period from June 4 to 28, Čabrinović found work at a printing shop and relaxed by taking walks through the city with the family's young dog. In conversations with acquaintances, he painted a rosy picture of his life in Belgrade (which contradicted his testimony at the trial). "He said that living was very inexpensive there, that there was freedom, that the people there have only one desire for Bosnia and Hercegovina, that they should be joined with Serbia," one witness recalled.[2] If nothing else, this period in Čabrinović's life shows how tenuous his involvement in the assassination appeared to be. Had his home life remained good for just a while longer he might have resisted the revolutionary call.

But it wasn't to be. He soon got into disputes with his father over staying out until nine or ten at night. "He didn't like it and scolded me. He is a man of hasty temper and that angered me, so I thought about going on somewhere else. All that time I thought about suicide."[3] As the day of the archduke's arrival in Sarajevo approached, father and son fought again, this time over the flags the former wished to display outside his house. At the interrogation Čabrinović said,

> Father wanted to hoist the Serbian and the imperial flags on our house, but could not find the flagpoles, although they had searched the whole house; I did not wish to tell them where the poles were. When my father started to curse my mother because of this, I thought it would be better for my father to hoist the imperial flag as well. At least I would not be suspected, and so I told him that the flagpoles were in the closet. At last my father put out the flags. When I reproached him for hoisting the imperial flag as well as the Serbian, he told me that he lived under this Emperor, that he esteemed him, that he was enjoying a good life, and if this house did not suit me I should look for a better place.[4]

It is ironic that the differences between father and son were due mainly to similarity of character. Both were emotional, hot-tempered, and prone to violent mood swings. Both were prone to suicidal thoughts: the elder Čabrinović attempted to take his own life on June 23, 1925, due to injustices committed against him, he said, and rumours he'd been an Austrian spy.

If Princip underwent any turmoil in the remaining weeks, it didn't involve his family. He smoothed things over with his brother with lies, assuring him he'd passed the eighth year of high school and saying he planned to take the matriculation exam in the fall. Much of his remaining days were spent reading and his evenings at Semiz's wine shop, where he drank wine for the first time in his life. At the interrogation he said he condescended to spend time with fellows who liked to drink and were "incapable of a great idea" because he needed a cover for his real purpose in Sarajevo.[5] In the last week before June 28, he worked as a secretary for Prosvjeta, which enabled him to return some of the twenty crowns he'd borrowed from Danilo Ilić to pay room and board.

While Čabrinović seems to have wavered in determination until more tumultuous dealings with his father pushed him toward carrying through with the plot, to the very end Princip appeared rock steady and ruthlessly decisive. Ilić, however, was suffering through an intense emotional and philosophical crisis. Increasingly his mind was divided between serious doubts about the tactical value of assassination in Bosnia-Herzegovina at the moment and the pressure to uphold his commitments to his colleagues and to conform with the identity he had built for himself. Instead of assassination as a trigger for revolution, he had come to advocate a progressive, organizational approach in advance of any final act of individual terror that would cause a revolution. He also believed, correctly, that Serbs would suffer because of the assassination, though he didn't think a world war would result. The problem for Ilić, though, wasn't purely theoretical. By this point he had a long track record of anti-Austrian plotting, befriending the main revolutionary figures of the time, as well as conceptually supporting assassination as a revolutionary tool. To back out now was virtually impossible from a personal standpoint.

But even had he wished to extricate himself, he knew he was in too deep in the eyes of the Austrian law. He had known about the attempt on Ferdinand's life from the get go (in fact, he was the principal organizer of the assassination); he had corresponded with the assassin, had picked up the weapons from Tuzla and hidden them in his mother's home, had set up a second troika (Mehmed Mehmebašić, seventeen-year-old Vaso Čubrilović, brother of Veljko, and sixteen-year-old Cvetko Popović); and he was rooming with the man who planned on killing Ferdinand.

Before any shot was fired, Ilić must have recognized the pressing danger to himself. At twenty-three, he was over the legal execution age of twenty. Afraid for his life, he must have wondered if it was worthwhile being linked to a crime that could have disastrous results.

Some of his actions suggest he attempted to thwart the assassination. Among the weak recruits of the second troika was young Popović who was too timid for the job and so near-sighted he said he couldn't see the archduke as he drove by. At the trial, Ilić said, "I did not say directly to Cubrilovic [sic] and Popovic [sic] that they should not perform the assassination, but I concluded that they were unfit for it."[6] Nor did Ilić allow the second group any practice time with the pistols, passing them out on the afternoon of June 27.[7]

Ilić made other attempts to prevent the assassination. In addition to telling Grabež directly not to carry it out, he attempted to dissuade Princip. "I talked with Princip as I also wanted to persuade him that there not be an assassination. I talked with him and he opposed it from the beginning, and later I said to him: let the other five do it, just you don't. Because I talked with him at length about that, he fell silent, but did not directly say: 'I won't,' but I understood that he agreed. I thought that he would not do it."[8] According to Čabrinović, Princip considered Ilić a snob because he didn't want to participate in the assassination. Despite the close confines of their room, Ilić and Princip were never farther apart. Princip grew silent because his mind was made up, steeled for his encounter with Ferdinand on June 28, and any further discussion was pointless.

If Ilić had considered the other assassins totally unreliable and believed he had convinced the most serious assassin, Gavrilo Princip, not to murder him, then why did he continue with the charade of organizing the assassins on the Appel Quay and distributing the weapons? Why put on this elaborate show if he hoped and believed it would fail?

Perhaps Ilić knew Princip hadn't changed his mind at all (though Ilić might have hoped his silence meant otherwise) and therefore felt pressured to continue or lose face with Princip and the revolutionary brotherhood to which they belonged. Unable to find a respectable way out of a precarious endgame and unwilling to risk flight and shame, he carried on. Had he known that in Vienna, shortly before the gunshots in Sarajevo, a secret conference of important South Slavic revolutionaries was preparing a declaration against political assassination, he might have found the moral support necessary to stop Princip. As it was, after years of talking revolution, he was finally forced to become a revolutionary in reality. Thus, his statements at the trial, while not entirely incorrect, were more the attempts at self-defense of a desperate man facing a death sentence for a crime he didn't really believe in. As Princip said, "I only know that I did not agree [with Ilić's advice]....It is his business to defend himself as best he can, but I say what I think."[9]

Another explanation for Ilić's continuation with the plot, despite earlier wavering, was the possibility of an order out of Belgrade. On June 15, members of the Black Hand's Central Committee got wind of Apis's support of the young Bosnians and ordered him to cancel the plan. Aware of Serbian Prime Minister Pašić's investigation of his activities, Apis sent word to Ilić through Major Tankosić's messenger, Đuro Šarac, who delivered the news at Bosanski Brod[10] on June 18. This would explain Ilić's reluctance to proceed with the plot after this date. However, Drago Ljubibratić says Apis's main intelligence operative in Bosnia, Rade Malobabić, who would be executed by his side in 1917, showed up at Ilić's house on the eve of June 28 with the order that the assassination should go ahead.[11] The likely reason cited was Apis's risky assumption that any attempt, even if it failed, would strain relations with his rival, the Serbian prime minister, and thereby strengthen his own position. At the trial, Ilić mentioned his concern about his personal safety if he did not carry on with the plans. "I was not allowed to take a forceful stand with respect to the assassination, because I knew myself that bombs came from Ciganovic [sic] and that Tankosic [sic] was the leader of the guerrillas. I was afraid that by my conduct I would become the object of open hostility."[12] If, however, the story of the first order from Belgrade were true, then Ilić's contention about reprisals against him doesn't carry any weight.

Although I tend to favour the first of these explanations, it's also possible that both personal and outside influences intertwined in Ilić's mind in the decisive days leading up to June 28. Ultimately, Danilo Ilić was a man more given to the study of philosophy and literature than to the "propaganda of the deed." Perhaps the most complex and misunderstood of the conspirators, his internal struggles and eventual fate make him one of the tragic figures in this story.

✦ Time was winding down inexorably to June 28. Archduke Ferdinand and his wife had arrived in Bosnia-Herzegovina, travelling by train to Sarajevo from the Adriatic coast. Whatever fears the heir had for his own safety due to Serbian unrest, he bravely dismissed. The closest to a specific warning about the plot against him—a veiled hint from the Serbian prime minister via the Serbian minister in Vienna, Jovan Jovanović-Pižon, to the Austro-Hungarian minister of finance that some young Serb might get a notion to fire a gun—probably never reached his ears.[13] After observing manoeuvres of the 15th and 16th Army Corps in the mountains southwest of Sarajevo, and after some sightseeing in Sarajevo, which included a visit to Baščaršija, the narrow warren of artisans' shops (where an armed Princip allegedly saw him but refrained from killing him for fear of hitting the duchess[14]), Ferdinand was set for his formal entrance in the capital.

Historians aren't certain who chose June 28 as the date for the archduke's arrival, and whether or not it was intended as a deliberate provocation to the Serbs or was just a colossal blunder. On both counts the decision seemed to bear the mark of Governor Oskar Potiorek, whose dislike for the uppity Serbs had been evident in certain policy decisions, such as the so-called "exceptional measures," which included the abolishment of various cultural associations. June 28, or *Vidovdan* (St. Vitus's Day), was a sacred day in the Serbian calendar, the anniversary of the Serbian defeat to the Ottomans in the Battle of Kosovo in 1389. Although historians have pointed out that the battle was less an outright defeat for the Serbs than a staging point for Ottoman dominance over the following decades (and indeed centuries)—and that the battle was not simply one between Serbs and Turks (for example, the Serb side also consisted of Albanians, Wallachians, Croats, Hungarians, and Bosnians)[15]—Serbs in 1914 viewed June 28 as a day of national consciousness.

At the heart of the Kosovo myth was Prince Lazar's speech to his men the night before the battle. One account of his words is as follows: "You yourselves are witnesses and observers of that great goodness God has given us in this life....But if the sword, if wounds, or if the darkness of death comes to us, we accept them sweetly for Christ and for the godliness of our homeland. It is better to die in battle than to live in shame. Better it is for us to accept death from the sword in battle than to offer our shoulders to the enemy. We have lived a long time for the world: in the end we seek to accept the martyr's struggle and to live forever in heaven. We call ourselves Christian soldiers, martyrs for godliness to be recorded in the book of life."[16] Lazar chose the eternal kingdom of heaven over the temporal kingdom of earth. One historian notes how the "real, lasting legacy [of the battle] lay in the myths and legends which came to be woven around it, enabling it to shape the nation's historical and national consciousness."[17]

Not only was the theme of self-sacrifice important to the assassins, but so was that of personal redemption, especially to Princip and Čabrinović. Princip had sought a chance to prove himself after the debacle with the Serbian *komite*, and Čabrinović, after being rejected by Princip and Grabež, drew parallels between himself and Miloš Obilić, who was accused by Lazar of betrayal on the eve of the battle, but who named Vuk Branković the true traitor and proclaimed his intention to prove his loyalty. He stole into the sultan's tent and stabbed him to death. Like Lazar, who was captured, he was executed by the Turks.

Both Princip and Čabrinović were ready to join the ranks of Serbian martyrs and die for the cause of Bosnian liberation. Princip embraced his destiny with fierce determination, though later he had some doubts about the cost, if his statements in prison are any indication. Čabrinović, after his final fight with his tyrannical father, suffered more deeply than Princip. In spite of his troubled home life and hard years on the road, he still loved life. But by the morning of June 28, his emotions had swung to the other extreme, and he made the irrevocable decision to leave his father's house for good. Although his mother was still upset with him because of his argument with her husband over the flags, he gave her his pocket knife as a memento. He gave his grandmother twenty crowns because, he said, he loved her and she'd always given him money when he was in need. Then he gave his sister, Jovanka, five crowns and told her they would never see each other again.[18] Alone in a room, he wept.

Once he'd closed the gate for what he thought was the last time and began walking into town, the dog appeared beside him. Stubbornly, it refused to obey his orders to go home, so he had to pick it up, carry it back, and lock it in the yard.

Čabrinović went to Vlajnić's cake shop at 8:15 A.M. and received a percussion bomb and cyanide from Ilić, but no Browning. "I didn't receive it at all," he recalled at the trial. "Ilic [*sic*] was convinced that I wouldn't carry out the assassination, so he didn't give it to me."[19] Similarly, Ilić only gave Grabež a pistol and a percussion bomb, but no cyanide, as though he didn't expect Grabež to need it. Maybe he had decided to withhold it at that last

Nedeljko Čabrinović and Tomo Vučinović. [from Dedijer, The Road to Sarajevo]

moment, because it was still in his pocket when he was arrested on the afternoon of June 28.

They said their last goodbyes then slipped into the street. Though still early, it was already very hot. The cries of hucksters floated out of the market as people went about their business as usual. Čabrinović walked around for a time until he met an old school friend of his, Tomo Vučinović. They chatted as though it were an ordinary day, and then he invited Tomo to accompany him to Schrei's photography shop in the Cirkus Square and asked him to pose with him for a portrait. As they sat together, he could feel the weight of the bomb in his suit jacket, and he fought off

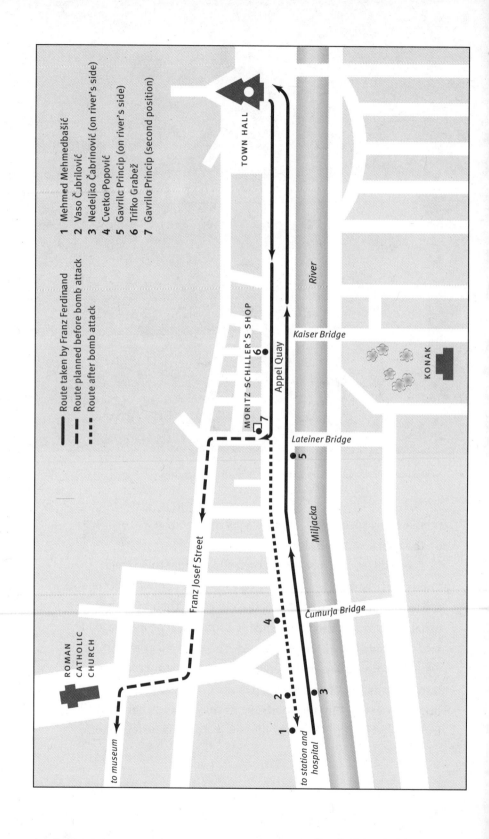

ROMAN
CATHOLIC
CHURCH

to museum

Franz Josef Street

to station and
hospital

1   Mehmed Mehmedbašić
2   Vaso Čubrilović
3   Nedeljko Čabrinović (on river's side)
4   Cvetko Popović
5   Gavrilo Princip (on river's side)
6   Trifko Grabež
7   Gavrilo Princip (second position)

— — Route taken by Franz Ferdinand
- - - Route planned before bomb attack
····· Route after bomb attack

TOWN HALL

River

Kaiser Bridge

MORITZ SCHILLER'S SHOP

Appel Quay

Lateiner Bridge

Miljacka

KONAK

Čumurja Bridge

the urge to take Tomo aside and show him. Saying he was leaving for Zagreb, he asked Tomo to send a copy of the photo to his grandmother, one to his sister, and the rest to friends in Belgrade, Trieste, and Zagreb, though some of the addresses were invented.

Once he had rid himself of Tomo, he went to the Appel Quay, the long avenue that runs beside the Miljacka River. Because the archduke was scheduled to drive down the Appel Quay on his way to the town hall, Ilić had decided to position all six of the assassins there. In order they were to be Mehmedbašić, Čubrilović, Čabrinović (who was to stand on the river side of the avenue), Popović, Princip (also on the river side), and finally Grabež. It isn't clear if Ilić's declared interest in foiling the assassination is evident in his plan or not. He placed the assassins on the most open part of the route where the crowds would be dispersed but where the motorcade would likely be travelling fastest, rather than on a narrow street where the cars would be forced to brake and turn but where the crowd could be heaviest. As it turned out, the conditions for an attempt on the archduke's life were relatively ideal; the motorcade wasn't speeding down the quay, the crowds were modest, and, most important, security was surprisingly thin.

Five of the six assassins failed to act on the archduke's first trip down the Appel Quay at 10:15 that morning. Mehemedbašić would later say he couldn't toss his bomb because a gendarme who happened to stand behind him would have grabbed his arm, revealed the plot, and prevented the other assassins from carrying it out. Čubrilović said his concern for the safety of the duchess prevented him from doing anything. Popović told a friend he couldn't see the heir in the first car because of his shortsightedness (the heir was in the third car), but during the trial he also admitted he was afraid. Princip said he couldn't pick out the archduke as the cars drove by. Finally Grabež offered various excuses for his failure, including his concern for the safety of the duchess and innocent bystanders, but also his lack of courage, according to his testimony at the investigation. Dedijer's attempt to save the reputation of Grabež by noting his "great *moral* courage" at the trial (when, by the way, Grabež offered yet more reasons for his inaction, claiming two detectives stood behind him, in addition to an acquaintance who might have become a suspect had he acted) doesn't convince me.[20] In short, Ilić's assessment of the conspirators was proven right.

When the motorcade approached Čabrinović, he turned to a policeman who had been standing nearby and asked him which car was the archduke's. Obligingly, the policeman pointed out a man in a cap with green feathers riding in a 1910 *Graef und Stift*. In light of the fact that Čabrinović had been recognized by police a few days earlier at the spa where the archduke and his wife had been staying, and had been identified as a "disturber," but allowed to go on his way, the policeman's response underscored once again the inadequate preparations for the heir's arrival in the capital.

Čabrinović pulled the bomb from his pocket and struck it against a light pole. The sharp sound was like a shot audible above the scattered shouts of *živio* (long live). Not waiting twelve seconds as he'd been taught by the *komite* in Belgrade, because the convoy would have gone by, he sent the bomb off early. The driver, noticing an object arc through the air, pressed on the accelerator. The bomb bounced off the folded roof of Ferdinand's car and clattered onto the street, exploding under the vehicle following behind. Ferdinand's piercing gaze turned to Čabrinović, who fell to the ground stuffing the cyanide into his mouth. Then he jumped from the sidewalk into the river below (a fact he proudly noted at the trial, contemptuously recalling that the others only slid down the embankment). Were his emotions at such a pitch that he reacted irrationally, or did he hope the fall would hasten his death? Whatever the reason, neither the fall killed him nor the river (which was only a foot deep), nor did the poison (which was old and only made him vomit). His attempt on the archduke's life had failed, but as he was apprehended in the water he yelled proudly, "I am a Serbian hero!" His pride was understandable; the conspirator everyone had dismissed as a joke and a liability had proven his mettle and had been the first to act.

In the chaos that followed, Princip, unaware that the attempt on Ferdinand's life had failed, thought of putting a bullet into Čabrinović's head then turning the gun on himself to keep the conspiracy secret. But he did nothing as the bloodied typesetter was led off.

✦ The archduke and his entourage made their way safely to the town hall where Sarajevo's Muslim mayor, who had been in the second car and had continued on while the heir's car had stopped, greeted them on the steps. Oblivious to the assassination attempt, he began his prepared speech, "Your Royal and Imperial Highness, Your Highness! Our hearts are full of happiness over the most gracious visit with which your Highnesses are pleased to honor our capital city of Sarajevo, and I consider myself happy that Your Highnesses can read in our faces the feelings of our love and devotion, of our unshakable loyalty...."[21]

This was too much for the archduke, and he tore into the hapless mayor, "What is the good of your speeches? I come to Sarajevo on a friendly visit and someone throws a bomb at me. This is outrageous."[22] His wife, Sophie, whispered something to him and he calmed down. "Now, you can get on with your speech."[23] This the timid, obedient mayor did, duly rattling off his speech without changing a word. When he finally arrived at the end of his last faltering sentence, Ferdinand addressed the group, remarking on the recent attempt against his life. When he finished talking, they all entered the town hall.[24]

While Sophie met a delegation of Muslim women upstairs, Ferdinand and his entourage discussed the assassination attempt and the steps they would take next. There was disagreement about what to do and where to go. Some were for cancelling the official visit altogether and leaving the country immediately via the nearest train station. Others suggested going to the governor's residence. But the archduke, ever the brave Austrian soldier, rejected these ideas and insisted on visiting a wounded member of his entourage—Lieutenant Colonel von Merizzi—at a military hospital. Shrapnel caused by Čabrinović's bomb had injured numerous people, including Sophie, who had been grazed slightly on the lower neck. Turning to Governor Potiorek, the archduke asked point blank whether any more attempts would be made against him. A reasonable man concerned about the welfare of the future emperor might have answered otherwise, but Potiorek was in a bind; he couldn't admit the security he'd provided was so ineffective and the country he governed so far out of his control that hordes of assassins lay in wait on the streets of Sarajevo. With the confidence of a man who hadn't been the target of a grenade attack, Potiorek assured the archduke, "Go at ease; I accept all responsibility."[25] He allegedly dismissed the suggestion of bringing troops in to line the streets because they wouldn't be attired in proper uniforms. But he did advise the archduke to cancel the scheduled visit to the museum and drive at high speed down the Appel Quay en route to the governor's residence for lunch or to Ilidže, where the couple had been staying. And so the decision was reached to dispense with added security and to travel down the Appel Quay on the way to the hospital. When Ferdinand informed his wife of this decision, she insisted on accompanying him rather than being escorted under protection to Ilidže.

In the meantime, Gavrilo Princip had heard that the assassination had failed and had walked to the corner of the Appel Quay and Franz Josef Street, where he expected the archduke's motorcade to turn in (based on the published itinerary). Had he looked down the quay he could have monitored the cars leaving the town hall, since the distance was no more than a few hundred metres. People walked by or waited in groups, discussing the failed attempt. In the excitement after Čabrinović's bomb, as he waited outside Moritz Schiller's shop, he must have felt a keen anticipation.

At the town hall, Ferdinand, Sophie, and Governor Potiorek climbed into the open car while Count Franz Harrach stood bravely on the car's left running board to shield the archduke from another attack from the river side. The motorcade departed Sarajevo's town hall and sped past thin pockets of bystanders, a few of whom waved in greeting. Seconds later, the chauffeur of the first car, a Czech named Leopold Sojka, turned in on Franz Josef Street, followed by the second car, and then Ferdinand's. For some reason no one had told the drivers of the change in plan! Maybe this was because the man who normally would have done so, the governor's aide, Lieutenant Colonel Merizzi, was at the hospital. The governor, noticing the mistake, shouted at the drivers, "What is this? This is the wrong way! We're supposed to take the Appel Quay!"[26] With this order he effectively handed Ferdinand over to his killer. By stopping and then reversing, the cars came to a standstill right in front of Gavrilo Princip.

Bested for the moment by his co-conspirator, Nedeljko Čabrinović—whom he'd later snidely dismiss as a "type-setter, not of sufficient intelligence"[27] to carry out an assassination—Princip was steeled for the arrival of the convoy a second time. People pressed from all sides, preventing him from pulling out the bomb. He chose the Browning instead, hesitating when he saw the white hat of a woman beside the heir. But a peculiar feeling, unlike anything he knew, impossible to express, caused him to act. "Where I aimed I do not know. But I know I aimed at the heir apparent. I believed that I fired twice, perhaps more, because I was so excited. Whether I hit the victims or not, I cannot tell, because instantly people started to hit me."[28] He tried to kill himself with his Browning but was prevented from doing so by a bystander. Like Čabrinović, he managed to swallow a dose of cyanide, which only made him sick.

Princip's two shots hit home. One struck Ferdinand in his neck, severing his jugular; the other lodged itself in the duchess's abdomen. For a moment both victims continue to sit as though nothing had happened. Then the duchess crumpled to the floor between the archduke's legs and said, "My God, what has happened to you?" The archduke sat stiffly upright, as though he were too proud to acknowledge an attack upon his person by a lowly Bosnian. Because Count Harrach still stood on the car's running board—on the wrong side as it turned out—he was able to hear the archduke plead, through the blood that choked him, "Soferl, Soferl, don't die, live for our children."[29]

✦ The site of the assassination is once again marked by a small plaque, informing visitors of the historical importance of the street corner, but the more partisan bas-relief of stylized figures, vaguely communist in appearance, with the words *Mlada Bosna* (Young Bosnia) engraved in Cyrillic, has been removed for good. You can still see the marks on the wall where the bas-relief used to be. Reuters announced in 2003 that Sarajevo would also restore the carved footprints that had long been embedded in the concrete at the site, ten years after they were destroyed, ironically, by Bosnian-Serb shelling. But the footprints were not there when I visited Sarajevo in 2006. Clearly, Sarajevo's Muslim authorities equated the young anti-Habsburgian revolutionaries with the Serbian nationalists who terrorized the city for three years.[30]

As I stood on the spot where the assassination took place, I saw people walk past without so much as a glance at the plaque or the "Sarajevo 1878–1918" museum. The museum, which used to be Moritz Schiller's delicatessen, was empty of visitors and devoid of any personal information about the assassins or their motivations. Replicas of the Browning[31] used by Princip hung inside a glass case, along with photos of the grenades and the trousers and bag Princip wore on June 28, 1914.

What struck me most about the corner was how tight it was, how easy it would have been physically for Princip to step off this sidewalk and shoot Ferdinand. However, I imagined that the

Site of the assassination.

assassination was more difficult psychologically. The intimacy of the moment must have affected even a decisive personality like Princip's, but a morbid yearning to kill Ferdinand had overcome him, and he was determined to go ahead. At the interrogation shortly after the assassination, he said, "Wherever I went, people took me for a weakling—indeed, for a man who would be completely ruined by immoderate study of literature. And I pretended that I was a weak person, even though I was not."[32] As Michael Pupin stated in comments published in the *New York Times* on June 29: "To men of mature years it is plain that nothing can be accomplished by murder, and such acts of lawlessness. But as that young lad standing in his cell tonight in Sarajevo he is smiling, he is happy. His instinct was to strike a blow for his country. And with his single arm he struck as high as he could hope to reach."

✦ The reaction to the assassination in Bosnia-Herzegovina was swift and violent. The Austrians arrested Serbs throughout the country, hanging many following sentences passed by special military courts. Once the war started, many Serbs were executed by new Austrian units called *Schutzcorps* without due process of law. By July 1914, roughly 5,000 Serbs languished in jails around the country. Pogroms against the Serbs were also carried out by Bosnian citizens. Many Croats and Muslims, either unaware of Princip's pan-Slavic or Yugoslav motivations, or simply attributing the assassination to a narrow Serbian nationalism, attacked Serbs in the streets and looted and burned Serb property. The looters were not only unemployed riff-raff with too much time on their hands but also more well-heeled citizens, among whom was one group that carried black flags and portraits of the deceased couple, sang the national anthem, and shouted *Živio* as they walked to the site of the assassination to pray. The city's best hotel, Sarajevo, owned by a Serb, was left in shambles, as were the offices of the two Serbian newspapers. The home and café belonging to Vaso Čabrinović, Nedeljko's father, were also vandalized. The violence was allowed to go on for an entire day until Governor Potiorek finally ordered martial law at four in the afternoon on June 29. This included a 9 P.M. curfew and a ban on Serb nationals travelling from Serbia.

In the end, Danilo Ilić's predictions about the suffering of the Serbs as a result of the assassination proved correct. But Ilić couldn't have predicted the catastrophe that was about to engulf the Western world. On July 28, 1914, exactly a month to the day after the assassination, Austria-Hungary declared war on Serbia after the Serbs accepted all the points in the ultimatum presented to them save one, number six, which demanded that a judicial inquiry be opened against those implicated in the murder, and to allow Austro-Hungarian agents to participate in the process on Serbian soil. The basis for the official Serbian repudiation of this demand was that it violated the Constitution and the Law of Criminal

Plaque on mausoleum that reads "Blessed is he whose name lives forever, a good reason had he to be alive."

Procedure. Despite Belgrade's conciliatory response (which satisfied Germany, Austria's closest ally), and its suggestion of referring the whole question to the International Tribunal at The Hague if Vienna remained dissatisfied, hawks in the Austro-Hungarian government won the day. A week later, the First World War began.

✦ When I arrived at Sarajevo's Lav Cemetery in June 2006 I saw some men gathered by the mausoleum where the principal Bosnian conspirators of 1914 were interred. A black plaque inscribed by silver letters informed me of their names: Gavrilo Princip, Danilo Ilić, Nedeljko Čabrinović, and Trifko Grabež.[33]

An older Serb I talked to, who wore a black suit and grey felt fedora, assured me that Princip's generation of young Bosnians was the best the country ever saw.

"Not all Serbs or all Bosnians would agree with you," I said.

"So let them disagree. I'm just saying that Princip's generation had honour. They had ideals. They wanted a South Slavic state free of the Austrians. Just compare them to the thugs who sat up in the hills here. I'm ashamed to call them my brothers."

Later, I met an elderly widow who was visiting the grave of her recently deceased husband. A tiny woman in a black shawl and kerchief, with little round blues eyes that shone like coloured glass in the sun, she'd lived all her life in Sarajevo (she was born there in 1930) but had never come to Lav Cemetery to pay her respects to the assassins.

Nevertheless I asked her what she thought of Gavrilo Princip and his colleagues.

"Oh, I think they were good. They loved Bosnia. They did what they did for all of Bosnia."

"But Princip killed a man and his wife. How can a man who kills be good?" I asked, recalling the *domaćin* in Mostar who had compared Princip with Osama bin Laden.

"Yes I know what they did, but to me they are good," she shrugged shyly, a little apologetically. "Such good boys," she added, smiling, as though she were talking about kids in her neighbourhood.

Like millions of students in both the first and second Yugoslavia, she'd learned to glorify the Young Bosnians. She couldn't remember any details about the conspiracy itself (indeed she knew little more than a few names and the basic facts), but what had stayed alive longer than anything else for her was the emotion at the core of the assassination, as though it had been distilled from all the impurities surrounding it. In this memory of hers, more emotional than factual, the love the conspirators said they bore the people of Bosnia-Herzegovina was as uncomplicated and undeniable as the fact of the assassination itself.

< *Mausoleum in Lav Cemetery where the assassins are interred.*

8 ✦ THERESIENSTADT

Records were kept of the assassins' statements from the moment they were arrested until their sentences were handed out and, in the case of Princip, even afterwards, when he was imprisoned in Theresienstadt. Besides the official minutes of the investigation and the trial (of which there are differing versions), there are the memoirs of individuals who met the assassins, such as that of the investigating judge, Leo Pfeffer. But as I learned, such first-hand accounts are often as dubious as they are valuable.

At 11:15 A.M., half an hour after firing his Browning, Princip was brought before Pfeffer. In his memoirs, published in 1938, Pfeffer recalled his first impressions of Princip, whose head was bandaged after his near lynching.

> *The young assassin, exhausted from his beating, could not speak a word. He was undersized, emaciated, sallow, sharp-featured. It was hard to imagine that such a frail-looking person could have committed so serious a crime. Even his clear blue eyes, burning and piercing, but serene, expressed nothing*

cruel or criminal. They signaled his innate intelligence, his steady and har-
monious energy. When I told him I was the investigating judge and asked
if he had strength to speak he answered my questions perfectly clearly in a
voice that grew steadily stronger and more assured.[1]

When Pfeffer first saw Čabrinović, he saw a tall young man
with lively black eyes, a bloody face, and a smirk on his lips.
Although Čabrinović never contradicted Princip's statement about
his Yugoslav motivations, he seemed to come at the assassination
from a different angle. He told the judge who first interviewed
him that he was a radical anarchist intent on destroying the
present constitutional order, and that Ferdinand was both a repre-
sentative of the existing system and also an enemy of the Slavs,
especially the Serbs. His admission about having arrived at the last
part of his conclusion by reading periodicals underscores the
naïvete and ignorance of the youthful assassins, who had been
swayed by anti-Habsburgian propaganda. They didn't know of the
archduke's opposition to war, his condemnation of Budapest's
treatment of the Croats, and his dabbling with the idea of
trialism.[2]

At first the two arrested assassins claimed to have acted on their
own. By July 2, after learning of the violence directed at innocent
Serbs, Princip asked to meet Danilo Ilić and Trifko Grabež so that
he could order them to divulge everything. Up to this point they
had both been silent about the conspiracy, even though Grabež
had been tortured. Čabrinović's statement during the trial—"I am
very pleased that there is no one in the prisoner's dock because
of me"[3]—appears critical of Princip and the others for divulging
secrets of the plot, although he seemed to have been responsible
partly for the arrest of Grabež due to his offhanded remark at his
father's café about travelling from Belgrade with *two* friends.
Princip also made a mistake early on when he registered with

> *Princip in his cell during the investigation.* [from Dedijer, Sarajevo 1914, p. 1011]

the police on his arrival in Sarajevo in June, naming Stoja Ilić's house as his place of residence. Once he was arrested he slipped again by saying he lived in the Ilić house and had done so when he first arrived in Sarajevo in 1907. Even though he tried to change the latter part of his story in the second hearing, it was too late. Danilo Ilić was arrested on the afternoon of June 28. For this reason, Princip's defense lawyer pointed out how Princip's confession "facilitated the inquiry and helped to find the other culprits Only after that was Ilic [sic] found out."[4]

Despite these facts, Ilić was named a traitor by some historians. According to Leo Pfeffer, Ilić was badly scared and tried to strike a plea agreement to save his skin. He promised to divulge everything if he would be spared the death penalty. Pfeffer said he couldn't promise anything, but he noted that courts had showed leniency in such cases before. No record of this conversation exists in the minutes of the investigation. Ilić's defense attorney, like Princip's, commended Ilić's confessions to police about the conspirators, but he went further and said his client eventually freed himself from Princip's authoritative personality. "[Princip's influence] continued after the assassination. Princip's intention was that some people remain hidden. I find it strange that precisely those people who were financially well off had to remain hidden. He intended to keep Misko Jovanovic [sic] hidden. When Princip was brought before the court he revealed where the bombs were and nothing else. Yet Ilic [sic] did not want to obey Princip any longer and told everything. That's why instead of four or five defendants you have 25. That is the result of Ilic's confession."[5]

Vladimir Dedijer doesn't acknowledge this rather damning statement, but he does argue that Pfeffer maliciously concealed the existence of the encounter between Princip, Ilić, and Grabež when Princip ordered them to reveal what they knew about the conspiracy; Pfeffer also didn't mention Princip's statement about his place of residence, nor did he mention other interviews given by Ilić on June 29 and 30, when he denied any knowledge of the plot. What were Pfeffer's motivations? According to Dedijer, "By 1938 the most chauvinistic elements in Yugoslavia were glorifying Princip, and Pfeffer, a conformist by nature, wanted to contribute to this attitude."[6]

The solution to this controversy about Ilić's behaviour during the investigation may be the misunderstanding or disagreement between him and Princip about how wide to cast the net after their encounter of July 2. Princip revealed only the main conspirators, while Ilić went further and betrayed Jovanović, as well as others. It is interesting that the man who was most reluctant to go ahead with the assassination was also the one to suffer the worst blows to his reputation afterwards.

The trial lasted from October 12 to 23, 1914. Altogether twenty-five accused were brought before the court to face charges. Besides the six assassins and Danilo Ilić, the accused included Mihajlo (Miško) Jovanović, Veljko Čubrilović, the peasants and agents who assisted the assassins in transporting the weapons, the students who had learned of the plot from their teenaged friends in the second troika, young Croat Ivo Kranjčević who had disposed of Vaso Čubrilović's unused Browning by wrapping it in cloth and handing it over to the mentally retarded sister of his relatives, and Kranjčević's relatives who were the victims of his foolish decision. The only Muslim in the conspiracy, Mehmed Mehmedbašić, fled to Montenegro, where he was arrested after boasting of his exploits but then "escaped." He would later be charged at Colonel Apis's Salonika trial in 1917 of having assisted Apis's right-hand man in Bosnia, Rade Malobabić, in an assassination attempt on Crown Prince Alexander Karadjordjević. The charges were probably invented, and judging by Mehmedbašić's track record when it came to assassinations, the attempt would probably have failed anyway.

The first to testify was Nedeljko Čabrinović. True to his nature, he was proud, emotional, argumentative, contradictory, and prone to occasional mental lapses. In his testimony he described his troubled past, particularly his fraught relationship with local authorities and with his father, his desperate period in Belgrade, his personal motivations for the assassination (which came across as more significant to him than his anarchism, which he'd cited at first), and other specifics of the plot. Once or twice he tangled with Princip; for instance, they disagreed about who came up with the idea for the assassination first. At one point, Čabrinović stumbled when he said no one in Serbia knew about the assassination except those few he had mentioned, and one of Tankosić's "friends." After Princip hastily stepped in and said the friend was a certain theology graduate called Kazimirović, Čabrinović burst out, "If you can prove to me that there was [another] person in Serbia who knew about it, you may tear me limb from limb."[7] It is tempting to conclude that here, for the only time in the trial, an allusion in Aesopian language was made to the shadowy Apis in Belgrade.[8] Another strange moment in Čabrinović's testimony was his comment about his peaceful character: "I would prefer if possible that there not be war, for I am a cosmopolitan and I do not wish to shed blood."[9] This statement seems laughable at first but has a certain logic once one understands that in Čabrinović's mind the archduke's supposedly tyrannical nature exempts him from these pious words.

Throughout his testimony, Princip wasn't as outgoing, emotional, or unsteady as Čabrinović, nor as likable. He was stern, forceful, absolute, and autocratic at times, withdrawn and sensitive at others. With his terse answers he gave the impression that he was irked by questions from a foreign-born prosecutor of an imperial court. While some of the accused were ready to ingratiate themselves with the judges or defend themselves against the charges of treason, like those men who faced the death penalty, Princip made no such efforts. Except his personal reasons for going first to Belgrade, which he refused to discuss, or the true nature of his fight with Čabrinović, or his rejection by the komite, his deceits were intended to help others. His claim he didn't know

Vladimir Gaćinović, his exchange about the friend of Tankosić's, which may or may not have concerned the head of the Black Hand, as well as his attempt to absolve the peasants by insisting he had threatened them, were cases in point. Once more he explained his political reasons for the assassination, which included his anger at the exceptional measures, the enlightenment of the people, and his view of Ferdinand as an "enemy of the Slavs" who would "introduce certain reforms, which...would be harmful to us."[10] He also cited as a reason for the assassination the indigent, oppressed state of the peasantry. "I am a villager's son and I know how it is in the villages. Therefore I wanted to take revenge, and I am not sorry."[11] For Princip this motivation was not abstract. But as one historian explains, the "idea of the peasantry has been enormously important as a resource in the construction of national mythologies throughout the entire region....Although the peasantry has been taken as the principal guarantor of the 'primordial' character of South Slav national identities, it has served this function passively, providing the symbolic resources out of which urban groups have constructed that vision of the primordial origins and entitlements of the nation."[12] For a while, Princip was the symbol for an indigent peasantry that actually acted on its outrage.

Unlike the haughty Princip, Danilo Ilić conducted himself with erratic desperation at the trial. His position from the start, even during the investigation when he disclosed secrets about the conspiracy, was an impossible one. For even in apparently doing himself good by outing the other conspirators, he admitted detailed knowledge about the plot, which in the eyes of the court was no different than if he had pulled the trigger himself. So as he tried to dig himself out, he actually dug his grave deeper. In general, his testimony turned into a prolonged attempt to show how he had tried to prevent the assassination and, secondly, to distance himself from statements he'd made at the investigation. For example, despite his statements concerning his conversations with Miško Jovanović about the assassination, which were quoted back to him, he prevaricated at the trial, saying, "Later I came to the conclusion that we two had absolutely not talked about the assassination. I don't recall what we talked about. We talked the most about the transportation of the bombs."[13] Then when he was asked to describe how he passed out the weapons and the poison to the two young members of the second troika, on the day before the assassination, he feebly tried to dodge the critical issue of having fired the Browning in a tunnel when he showed the students how it worked. Said the prosecutor, "Because you have fooled around enough today, say whether it is true , whether you, when you gave the revolvers to Cubrilovic [sic] and Popovic [sic], showed them how to shoot those revolvers in a tunnel?" His first answer was, "I don't remember now. I think I didn't," and then a more categorical "I didn't," and finally, "It is possible, I admit it."[14] Neither Popović nor Čubrilović assisted him; the latter, especially, was motivated to clear himself of the charge of having fired his revolver when the bomb was thrown (he'd boasted to a friend that he had). What Ilić didn't deny was quoting a line from a folk song, "*Dje udari melem ne trebuje*" ("Where you apply this medicine you're really cured").[15] The prosecutor pointed out Ilić's hopeless situation: "You said ['that is for poisoning'] to them the day before the assassination and gave them arms, and now you want to say that you withdrew from the assassination."[16]

In his first letter to his mother while in prison, Ilić acknowledged his dire situation. "I may be sentenced to death." He also told her to request the return of her money, which had been taken from her house, and to bring him his winter coat and socks. "If you cannot come, you write, if you are well and if your house is still in one piece and if they gave you the money back." His final letter, written from his solitary cell two weeks before his execution, reads as follows. "Dear mother I am well and healthy. Do not be very sad because I hope that my thing will end well and soon too. As soon as you get my letter bring me forty crowns here and give them to the office, and I don't need any change of clothes. Say hello to my aunt. Greetings, Danilo."[17]

One of the most memorable moments of the trial came when the court heard Count Harrach's account of the archduke's last words to his wife. Everyone in the courtroom was moved and the defendants lowered their heads. When Princip's defense attorney asked what he thought of the heir's words, Princip retorted by asking whether the man thought he was a beast.

Another emotional moment took place toward the very end of the trial, when Čabrinović stood up and passionately explained the position of the assassins.

> Before we part I should like to express the wish that you understand us, that you not consider us criminals. We love our people. Nine-tenths of our people are farm workers. They scream, live in misery, they have no schools, no culture. It hurt us. We felt the anguish of our people. We did not hate the Habsburg dynasty. Although I nourished anarchistic ideas, although I hated everything, never in a single thought was I against his Highness Franz Josef. The only thing I did not like was that he received 60,000 crowns per day. We did not plan this assassination of Franz Ferdinand. We admitted that this idea did not arise in our minds. In the society in which we lived there was always talk of assassination....[T]he people we (lived) among talked about Franz Ferdinand, they regarded him as an enemy of the Slavs. We heard of him that he was an enemy of the Slavs. Nobody told us directly: "Go kill him," but in that milieu we came to that idea.
>
> There is still something else I would like to say. Although Princip plays the hero, although all of us play the hero, nevertheless we are very sorry, because we did not know, in the first place, that the late Franz Ferdinand was the father of a family. We were deeply touched by the words which he said to his late wife: "Sophie, stay here, live for our children." Think what you like of us, but we are not criminals. For myself and in the name of my comrades I beg that the children of the late Heir Apparent forgive us; and

you render whatever verdict you like. We are not evildoers, we are honest
people, honorable, idealistic, we wanted to do good, we loved our people, we
will die for our ideals.[18]

After the trial, the head of the Jesuits in Sarajevo, formerly the
father-confessor of Franz Ferdinand, Father Anton Puntigam,
who had heard the entire trial, visited Čabrinović in his cell with
a letter from Ferdinand and Sophie's children. They forgave him
because he had expressed his regret for the death of their parents.

Princip's proud nature couldn't allow Čabrinović the last word.
Nor could he let him imply that the assassination, which he had
carried out after all and was about to suffer the consequences for,
originated with anyone other than with him and his Bosnian conspirators. Typical of his terse, imperturbable character, his final
words lack the emotional power of Čabrinović's, though to his
credit he knew better about the people's misery because he had
experienced it himself. "If they want to impute that someone else
was the instigator, then I must say that that is not true. The idea
grew in us, so we carried out the assassination. We loved our people. I do not want to make any other statement in my defense."[19]

Despite the relatively free reign permitted the accused to defend
themselves as they wished and to speak their minds, the verdict
for this show trial was preordained. The half-hearted efforts of
some of the defense lawyers reflected this reality. For instance,
although counsellor Štrupl said he would speak mainly in defense
of his client, Trifko Grabež, his statement consisted of only forty-
four words in the English translation, and he spent much more
energy on Mićo Mićić, the courier on the island in the Drina, than
he did on his primary client. The defense lawyer for Čabrinović,
Jovanović, and Mitar Kerović, a Croat named Dr. Konstantin
Premužić, began by admitting how difficult it was for him to
defend Serbs, especially those who killed the heir to the empire on
whom the Croats had pinned their greatest hopes for some form of
independence. The most effective defense was made by Dr. Rudolf

Cistler, the lawyer for Veljko and Vaso Čubrilović, Ivo Kranjčević, and Nedjo Kerović. More than the other members of the court, he was conscious of his legal obligations and the trial's importance to history. He argued that because the annexation of Bosnia-Herzegovina had never been ratified in the Austro-Hungarian legislative assemblies in Vienna and Budapest, the country still existed as a separate entity, a fact that disqualified the charge of high treason. Naturally, this argument was untenable in the eyes of the court, which intended to see someone hang, even if it wasn't the assassin himself (who was nineteen at the time of the assassination[20]) or the other students under the age of twenty. For his troubles, Cistler was banished from Sarajevo after the trial.

The verdict was delivered on October 28. Princip received "penal servitude for a period of 20 (twenty) years, intensified by one day of fasting each month and one day of solitary confinement in a darkened cell on June 28th of each year."[21] Čabrinović and Grabež received the same sentence, though the former was spared the fast, and the latter received the fast every three months. Vaso Čubrilović got sixteen years confinement at hard labour with a day of fasting every six months and solitary confinement in a darkened cell every June 28; and Popović got thirteen years penal servitude and solitary confinement in a darkened cell every June 28. Ilić, Veljko Čubrilović, and Jovanović were sentenced to death by hanging, which was duly carried out on February 3, 1915, despite petitions for amnesty by family members. The authorities added to Ilić's mental suffering by making him last in the queue.[22]

✦ In the rolling flatlands sixty kilometres northwest of Prague lies the former military fortress and garrison town of Theresienstadt. Founded by Josef II of Austria in 1780, and named after his mother, Empress Maria Theresa, it eventually became a notorious transit camp under the Nazis.[23]

I went to Terezin (the prison's name in Czech) in June 2006 to finish the last stage of my journey.

After a drive through pleasant farmland and fallow meadows of tall swaying grass, I came first to the small fortress—a long, low-lying structure of mouldering brick protected by a moat. The main fortress, in which the town of Terezin itself is situated, was farther on. Exiting the town to the north, the walls of the fortress came at the road at sharp angles, and the roofs were thatched with grass and sprinkled with dandelions, clover, and daisies. Many of the town's crumbling buildings were boarded up, and few people were on the streets. Built monotonously of the same brick as the fortresses, Terezin was a dead town with a heavy atmosphere and a deteriorated yet unmistakable air of military power. Now that this military past was over (the Czech army left in 1996), Terezin was struggling to find a new identity among the ghostly ruins left behind.

In the parking lot near the small fortress, students out of tour buses crowded around food stands and a gift shop, which sold souvenirs like glasses, plates, and key chains. I walked under a majestic canopy of trees along a cobbled lane that led me to the small fortress. It was a beautiful entrance to an otherwise grim place. Once inside the main walls of the prison, I saw the notorious Nazi motto painted above the interior gate: *Arbeit Macht Frei*.[24] Seeing the sign sent a tremor through me, but another feeling, a growing anticipation and excitement, soon took hold. I was finally nearing the end of my journey, the cell in which the assassin I'd been pursuing for so long was imprisoned. All else, all the suffering of victims in Theresienstadt during the Second World War, waned in importance to me as I made my final stop.

Another left turn took me into the courtyard where the isolation cells were located, all of them built inside the fortress' outer wall. The roof of the prison was thatched with grass and studded with white flowers. A plaque outside read "Princip's cell" in Czech, while another in the corridor, placed there by the Yugoslav

< Entrance to the small fortress, Terezin.

Cellblock #12. Right: Princip's cell.

government in 1953, informed me that "Gavrilo Princip was imprisoned and tortured here."

A lamp was set up inside the first cell on the left, I noticed, as I stepped into a cramped rectangular space, around eight feet by four, with a partially coved ceiling, a tiny rectangular air hole above the door, and a metre-high curved grate in the corner that served as a wood stove fed from outside. The cell floor was faded hard wood that bent under my weight. I saw an iron coil attached to the far wall, to which prisoners were chained by shackles weighing ten kilos.

The shackles had been removed and the walls recently painted white, except where the bricks showed through, as part of

renovations to the prison after a flood in 2002 that had devastated the region. This tidied cell wasn't quite the dungeon I had expected. And yet I felt closer to the ghost of Princip than ever before. Nowhere in all of Bosnia-Herzegovina had I occupied a space that had enclosed his elusive presence. In cell #1 I felt the killer breathe; I sensed the walls press on him as they did on me now.

But I hadn't got close enough; I went into the neighbouring cell and shut the door on myself to get a feeling for the nights and for those hours when the dim light was turned off.[25] I sat against the far wall where the shackles used to be and breathed in the dank air. Even though the main door of the cellblock was open, letting daylight into the hallway, the cell was almost completely dark. The air hole was a shade lighter than the surrounding darkness, and my eyes automatically turned to it, as his must have, for a sign of the guard's arrival.

The ground pressed against me, and I shifted once to get comfortable then tried lying on the wooden floor. It was no better, though he must have gotten used to the hardness of the floor and the wooden cot, because he was able to sleep and even to dream. The main problem was staying warm, as the grate went unheated and the water in the jugs froze.

Maybe, like fellow inmate Ivo Kranjčević, the young Croat who had helped hide Čubrilović's pistol, Princip learned to conserve his heat by wrapping himself around the shackles. Wrote Kranjčević: "At first I did not know how to protect myself from them. The first winter I left the shackles outside my bed. The chain thus sucked the warmth from my body, and in the morning I was frozen stiff and had great difficulty standing up. The second winter I realized that I should bring the chain into bed and warm it with my hands, so that it remained warm all night and did not lead my heat away."[26]

Between long, silent intervals the door opened and Princip was allowed a solitary, half-hour stroll in the courtyard. Walking back and forth he would have been able to see the sky and the grass roof of the prison. In all likelihood he carried out a pail and dumped his waste.

Princip's prison was as much his body as his cell. Due to the grinding brutality of each day in Terezin, the tuberculosis that had likely invaded him before 1914 began to ravage his body. His left forearm withered to a stump and was kept attached by a wire (according to one report), until doctors decided to amputate.

But if solitary confinement limited Princip to the extreme physically, it opened the vistas of his interior life. He escaped Terezin each day, fighting alongside fellow Serbs who were losing to the Austro-Hungarian army, as his jailors were happy to inform him (better news from the front was smuggled into his cell on the handle of a shaving brush by a Polish barber called Spak). In his thoughts, Princip also went home and visited his family. He told psychiatrist Martin Pappenheim, who interviewed Princip four times in 1916 and who took stenographic notes, that he frequently "thinks of his parents and all, but hears nothing. Confesses longing. That must exist in everyone." At night he had beautiful dreams, as though his mind tried to compensate for the pain of his waking hours. Dreams "about life, about love, not uneasy," he told Pappenheim. Asked what else he though about, Princip said his thoughts varied. "Sometimes in a philosophical mood, sometimes poetical, sometimes quite prosaic. Thinks about the human soul. What is essential in human life, instinct, or will, or spirit— what moves man?"

Solitary confinement was "very hard," he said, "without books, with absolutely nothing to read and intercourse with nobody." Indeed, the four visits by Pappenheim amounted to the most social interaction he had during the final years of his life. In reading Pappenheim's account, though, one gets the impression that Princip kept his most private thoughts close to his chest, as he had throughout the trial. The first interview took place on February 19, 1916. Princip told the psychiatrist his shackles had been removed for the first time three days before. He also divulged a few spare details about his "ideal love" with an unnamed girl in 1911. He said they had "never kissed," but then shut the door on Pappenheim and revealed no more.[27] Simultaneous with this first stirring of the heart was the awakening of his political ideals. The shortfall between these ideals and the reality on the ground after a year and a half of war caused him mental pain. "Has heard a tragic thing, that Serbia no longer exists. His life is in general painful, now that Serbia no longer exists. It goes hard with my people."[28] He also mentioned an attempt at suicide, using a towel to hang himself.

The second interview occurred on May 12, 1916, in the prison hospital where Princip had been transferred because of deteriorating health. "He recognizes me immediately and shows pleasure at seeing me. Since 7 IV here in hospital. Always nervous. Is hungry, does not get enough to eat. Loneliness. Gets no air and sun here; in the fortress took walks. He no longer has any hope for his life. There is nothing for him to hope for. Life is lost."[29] He seemed less distressed when he remembered his revolutionary past. "But for such a revolution one must prepare the ground, work up feeling. Nothing happened. By assassination this spirit might be prepared. There already had been attempts at assassinations before. The perpetrators were like heroes to our young people. He had no thought of becoming a hero. He wanted merely to die for his idea."[30]

When Pappenheim interviewed Princip a third time on May 18, 1916, his large tubercular sores were discharging freely. In comparison to his pain now, the psychological suffering he underwent because of the condescending attitude of others was more a point of fact than deeply felt. "Many who have spoken with him think he is a child, think that he was inspired by others, only because he cannot express himself sufficiently, is not in general gifted as a talker. Always a reader and always alone, not often engaging in debates."[31] As though to compensate again for this view of himself, Princip reiterated his assertion that the assassination was his idea. Now that his rival, Nedeljko Čabrinović, had succumbed to tuberculosis, malnutrition, and the pain of solitary confinement on January 23, 1916, Princip could make this boast without being contradicted. Never in these interviews was he to show any affection for his former co-conspirator. The "friendly" argument with Čabrinović on the road to Sarajevo was one they never really forgot. For Danilo Ilić, however, his "best friend," Princip showed fondness, though he thought Ilić had grown a "little lightheaded" when he discussed his pan-Slavist ideas[32] and had come under his influence, even though he was older. Pappenheim's final interview with Princip on June 5, 1916, was a brief one. "When permission has come, arm is to be amputated. His usual resigned disposition."[33]

Although conditions in Terezin appeared to improve slightly as time wore on, maybe because the regime was staring down defeat and was ready to make peace, Princip didn't survive his sojourn there. In the prison hospital, with hope for life gone, he wished only to return to his cell where at least he would be permitted to see the day.

I went back to Princip's cell and thought for a moment of the men, before and after, who served their terms or lived out their last days in his cell. Many will remain nameless and forgotten. It struck me as a quirk of history that the assassin who triggered the First World War was held in the same cell as victims of the second.

What, in the end, did Princip think of his assassination of Franz Ferdinand? From Pappenheim's spare notes one detects a change of attitude. His original motives, he said, were revenge and love—revenge against the Habsburgs for their occupation of Bosnia-Herzegovina, and love for the people. By the time he spoke to Pappenheim, however, his intractable conviction, though always tempered by regret for having accidentally killed Ferdinand's wife, seemed to relent. While once he had followed through on anarchistic pamphlets inciting political murder, he acknowledged the shortcomings of that approach. A "revolution especially in the military state of Austria, is of no use." He went on to tell Pappenheim that he "cannot believe the World War was a consequence of the assassination; cannot feel himself responsible for the catastrophe; therefore cannot say if it was a service. But fears he did it in vain." Proud to the end, Princip refused to admit openly that Ilić had been right to dissuade him from action in the days leading to June 28. Perhaps to say so would have left Princip with nothing, and he couldn't manage such a step.

Princip's body was buried secretly on the night of his death in a Catholic cemetery. One of the four Austrian soldiers responsible for this duty, a Czech named František Löbl, sketched a map of the location and after the war placed a Czech flag on the grave. The remains of Princip, Čabrinović, Grabež, and the other conspirators who had died in Theresienstadt and Möllersdorf were transferred to Sarajevo and, along with Ilić, Veljko Čubrilović, Jovanović, and Bogdan Žerajić, were buried in a common grave.

The rest is silence. Except for these words that Princip allegedly scratched on the wall of his cell in the first months of his imprisonment:

Our ghosts will walk through Vienna
And roam through the Palace, frightening the lords.[34]

✦ CONCLUSION

AFTER MY FATHER AND I LEFT TREBINJE, we crossed the Croatian border where the road descended through spacious rolling country toward the Adriatic. Far below, covered in a haze, a few islands floated in the pale blue space where the sea met the sky. Warm spring air blew through our open windows, carrying a faint aroma of curry from a yellow herb in the stony fields.

Looking down at the Adriatic, the blue shoulder of Bosnia-Herzegovina behind me, I felt a relaxed feeling I can only describe as relief. After years of toiling on a story that had fascinated, obsessed, and appalled me, casting a long shadow over my mood, I was ready to leave Bosnia for good.

The first stage of our trip home took us along the southernmost stretch of the Magistrala Highway, which winds along Croatia's Adriatic seaside and past its most spectacular city, Dubrovnik. For the first time my father asked me to stop so he could take

The author by the bridge on the Drina in Višegrad. [photo by Josip Fabijančić]

some pictures. Later, we had lunch in Tučepi, a resort town with an atmosphere so innocuous and blandly pleasant I thought I'd arrived in another world. Diving into the water, I felt as though I were washing something off.

But it didn't come off. The spectres of Gavrilo Princip and Bosnia hung over me stubbornly throughout the bright summer. They haunted my best moments, the pleasurable distractions of everyday life. Lying on a beach in Nova Scotia, watching my kids play, I suddenly saw the gaunt ravaged body in its dark cell, and I felt its disease. True, I hadn't been through a war or a traumatic experience, but I couldn't rid myself of the feeling that I knew something that the people around me, living their ordinary lives, couldn't understand. I laughed at the intellectual vanities and self-important rantings of my colleagues. When I met my first-year students, I compared them secretly to the Young Bosnians.

But in time all this started to fade, and I gradually began to lose touch with the assassins, their story, and indeed all of Bosnia. Looking back, I could trace my relationship with Princip and the Young Bosnians clearly, and for the first time in its entirety; I'd gone from the respect and support I'd felt for Princip at the start of my travels, to disgust at the criminal form his Serbian-led Yugoslav nationalism took during the war of the 1990s, to a certain sympathy for the young, naïve idealist, in the context of a deeper understanding of the Bosnian *gestalt*. The Princip I knew at the end was a weaker, more human, more fleshed-out version of the ghost I knew at the beginning. I never went so far as to share the message of photographs in the Serbo-Croatian version of Vladimir Dedijer's book, where sunbeams above Princip's hamlet, Gornji Obljaj, shine gloriously through storm clouds. Most Bosnians, even many Serbs, would have trouble grasping the emotional idealism of those images.

Gavrilo Princip, I have decided, is a subject about which Bosnians will either remain uninformed or about which they will always disagree. Those who have tapped into their storehouse of national memories and have found evidence for differing interpretations of the assassin, even those who agree on a starting point, soon get caught up in the fraught terrain of their own history. To some extent Princip has become exemplary of the process in Bosnia whereby the concrete realities of history are distorted, forgotten, abstracted, and ultimately used by various groups to suit their narrow interests.

If the past is so undefined and open to argument, what about the future of Bosnia-Herzegovina? More pessimistic than when I first arrived there, I have come to the conclusion, as my father did, that despite claims about multi-ethnic harmony, the old animosities continue. A Croat I met captured the reality of Bosnia's social relations when he said that the Serb he worked with would never know how much he hated Serbs and that he was friendly only because they had to work together. This kind of superficial politeness, which hides deeper feelings of mistrust and even hatred, often passionate and irrational, prevailed over ethnic bloodletting for centuries. What set things off in Bosnia in the 1990s continues to live on under the surface, biding its time. In contrast, the assassination in 1914 was, conceptually at least, an attempt to unite Bosnians rather than to divide them.

Now as I read over these last words, a year and a half removed from my last visit to Bosnia, I am eager to end this story. As the snow falls heavily outside my window, onto the rink that has taken over my life this winter, I have a sense of the things that were lost rather than gained by Princip's assassination.

On my desk is a letter from one of the conspirators, Veljko Čubrilović, to his daughter, a letter that has sat under piles of papers and books for months until it reappeared recently, as if by design. Čubrilović wrote the letter the day before his execution.

My darling only child,

Many years will have passed by the time you read this letter. A little bud will have grown into a beautiful blossom. The little Nada whose picture is before me will have grown into a fine girl. Your father can imagine you as a young woman, full of modesty, that most gracious quality of girlhood; quiet and calm, thoughtful and intelligent. My child, the only thing that your father can leave you is his honest and untarnished name. He remains in your debt; but he leaves you his great love and his unblemished name.

Toward the end of his letter, in speaking of the political turmoil that led to his death sentence, he offered some parting advice. Sadly, though he spoke from his heart, he voiced sentiments that have been the cause of so much grief in the long troubled history of Bosnia-Herzegovina.

Now you are already grown up and can understand those tumultuous times in which your father lived and, if you can understand them, you will forgive him....Be honest. And love the people whose roots are your own.[1]

✦ NOTES

PREFACE

1. In Vladimir Dedijer, *The Road to Sarajevo* (New York: Simon and Schuster, 1966), 193.

INTRODUCTION

1. The empire had been permitted to occupy Bosnia in 1878 at the Congress of Berlin, which had been convened to settle the crisis in the Balkans after the *kmetovi* (serfs) of Herzegovina rebelled against their living conditions under the Ottomans. Barbara Jelavich points out that the military occupation was carried out by divisions of the Croatian Thirteenth Army Corps, based in Croatia, under General Josip Filipović: "He set up a provisional government, staffed largely by Croatian civil servants, and the laws and legal system of Croatia were introduced. As could be expected, Croatian opinion was most enthusiastic about the occupation. It was hoped that the territory would be joined to Croatia's, an action that was essential for Croatian national aims." Barbara Jelavich, *History of the Balkans, Twentieth Century, Volume 2* (Cambridge: Cambridge University Press, 1983), 61. The Austrians played Croats against Serbs, as well as Christian groups against Muslims, as a way of bolstering

their authority. Serbs in Bosnia fumed at the Austrian presence, but Serbia itself was angry because its access to the sea would be cut off. See Eterovich, Francis H. and Christopher Spalatin, eds., *Croatia: Land, People, Culture, Volume I* (Toronto: University of Toronto Press, 1970), 51.

2. The annexation was an immediate cause of the founding in November 1908 of a Serbian nationalist organization called *Narodna Odbrana* (National Defense), which turned to cultural matters following Serbia's official recognition of the annexation of Bosnia-Herzegovina. This ready capitulation to outside interests saw the rise of the Black Hand, which assimilated the *Narodna Odbrana*'s agents and covert operations throughout Bosnia-Herzegovina. The Black Hand was an illegal association in a constitutional parliamentary democracy like Serbia's. It was modelled on the Freemasons, the Italian Carbonari, Guiseppe Mazzini's Young Italy movement, the Burschenschaften movement in Germany, and radical terrorist groups like the People's Will and the Bulgarian Internal Macedonian Revolutionary Organization (IMRO). Like the *Narodna Odbrana*, it had a pan-Serbian programme. "This organization prefers terrorist action to intellectual propaganda, and for this reason must be kept absolutely secret from non-members" (q. Stavrianos 550). According to David Mackenzie, "after 1912 [the] 'Black Hand' in Serbia advocated Greater Serbian leadership or domination over other South Slavs whereas 'Young Bosnia' favored an egalitarian Yugoslav federation." David Mackenzie, *The "Black Hand" on Trial, Salonika, 1917* (Boulder, CO: East European Monographs, 1995), 44. Initially in 1911–1912 it had elements of a pro-Yugoslav orientation that "yielded during its second, intolerant phase, 1913–14, to bellicose chauvinism" (Mackenzie 47).

3. The first of Emperor's Franz Josef's heirs to die prematurely was his younger brother, Ferdinand Maximilian Josef, who accepted the imperial crown of Mexico from a group of wealthy Mexican landlords, with Napoleon III in support. Benito Juarez, the liberal opposition leader in Mexico, aided by the United States, rebelled against the Habsburg, and eventually captured, court-martialled, and executed him by firing squad. The second heir to die was Franz Josef's son, Rudolf, who died in a shooting lodge on January 30, 1889. The third was the emperor's second-youngest brother, the father of Franz Ferdinand, Archduke Karl Ludwig.

4. L.S. Stavrianos, *The Balkans Since 1453* (New York: Rinehart, 1961), 546.

5. Sophie Chotek was born in Stuttgart on March 1, 1868. Although of Czech descent, her native tongue was German.

6. Gavrilo Princip's fellow assassin Nedeljko Čabrinović, basing his views on slim evidence from some vaguely remembered newspaper article, believed military manoeuvres in Bosnia were a prelude to an attack on Serbia itself.

But it was not only teenagers like Čabrinović who appeared to misinterpret Ferdinand's intentions; respected newspapers around the world had come to the same conclusion. A headline in the June 29, 1914, *New York Times* stated that "His Designs on Slavic Territory Had Long Threatened To Bring About Trouble."

7. In Dedijer, *The Road to Sarajevo*, 136–37.

8. In Dedijer, *The Road to Sarajevo*, 190.

9. Gavrilo Princip, *The Sarajevo Trial, Volume I*, ed. W.A. Dolph Owings, trans. Owings, Elizabeth Pribic, and Nikola Pribic (Chapel Hill, NC: Documentary Publications, 1984), 57.

10. In October 1912, Montenegro and Serbia declared war on Turkey and, with Bulgaria and Greece, drove the Turks out of the Sandžak, Novi Pazar, Kosovo, and Macedonia. Most zealous youths fired up by these victories probably didn't know that the Serbs and their allies slaughtered Muslim-Albanian villagers, drove out tens of thousands of Slavic Muslims from Macedonia, and committed Bulgarian Muslims to forced conversions.

11. Princip's assassination of Franz Ferdinand, because it was both a blow struck on behalf of Bosnian independence from foreign occupation *and* a step toward the country's *absorption* into a wider South Slavic state, gets to the heart of a longstanding tension in the country between unity and division. Of all the republics in the former Yugoslavia, Bosnia has had the longest history as a state, kingdom, or republic, and yet it has also been the fulcrum of a battle for its partition, sought both by forces within and those outside. As early as the fourteenth century, Stjepan Tvrtko emerged from Bosnia's fractious nobility and declared himself king of Bosnians and Serbs, holding the semblance of a fragile kingdom together until his death. A kind of anachronistic "national consciousness" seemed to have existed in the form of the medieval Bosnian Church, which signalled a desire among some Bosnians for a vernacular-based Christian faith separate from Rome. And the war in the 1990s was fought mainly on the issue of the territorial integrity of Bosnia (as against its inclusion in a greater Serbia or Croatia). But Bosnia has been afflicted by certain weaknesses that prevented any long-lasting independence. One of the various nails in the coffin of Bosnian autonomy was the centrifugal effect of the nobility, who wielded great power and made the central authority ineffective. Another was the country's mountainous terrain, which, while it made invasions harder, made travel, business, and the maintenance of centralized order almost impossible. Most important, Bosnia lacked a common faith (and the attending ethnicity) to bind the state together (rival Orthodox and Catholic churches, the Bosnian Church, the Bogomil heresy, and Islam). To sum up, the disunity of the

South Slavs throughout history meant they couldn't be as dominant as their numbers suggested.

12. The interrelationship among Bosnians has been viewed by historians as either one of relatively peaceful coexistence or constant strife, segregation, and hatred. The latter view was given popular credence by Western politicians loath to intervene in the Yugoslav wars of the 1990s. Happy to tiptoe around calls for intervention, leaders like British Prime Minister John Major cited unsolvable "ancient ethnic hatreds" as reason enough to stay out of the conflict. In contrast, some academics went to the other extreme and painted a picture of a Bosnian utopia where multicultural harmony and intermarriage were constants. Rightly, they called the phrase "ancient ethnic hatreds" anachronistic since Bosnian identity in the premodern period was mainly based on religion, but they went further and said Bosnians were never motivated by ethnicity when committing violence against one another. See Robert J. Donia and John V.A. Fine Jr., eds., *Bosnia and Hercegovina: A Tradition Betrayed* (London: Hurst and Company, 1994). It is true that Bosnia-Herzegovina has often been a violent place, that ethnic cleansing practices by Serbs took place in Bosnia against Muslims between 1804–1815, that blood feuds, the practice of mutilation of dead and wounded opponents, the depiction of heroism in traditional oral epic poetry, all testify to ethnic violence in Bosnian history. And yet, as some historians have pointed out, Bosnia's history is probably no more violent than, say, France's. And no Western politician would accuse the French of "ancient ethnic hatreds." Throughout the long centuries of Turkish rule people may not have loved one another, but they cohabited in most Balkan towns and villages, practiced tolerance and, occasionally, co-operation. This mutual tolerance was ruined by the arrival from Europe of nationalist ideas that the new Balkan intelligentsia foisted onto peasants (and, one might add, youths), who interpreted them in an unsophisticated fashion. See Misha Glenny, *The Balkans: Nationalism, War and the Great Powers 1804–1999* (New York: Viking, 1999). For a summary of these arguments and a fine review of Glenny's book, as well as John Allcock's *Explaining Yugoslavia* (New York: Columbia University Press, 2000), and Mark Mazower's *The Balkans: A Short History* (New York: The Modern Library, 2000), see Richard Crampton, "Myths of the Balkans," *The New York Review of Books* (January 11, 2001): 14. Another common view about social relationships in Bosnia, especially among foreign writers on the former Yugoslavia, is that the violence throughout the centuries was often the result of outside, imperial incitement. There is plenty of evidence for this view, especially in the Austro-Hungarian period. For example, Austrian statesman Count Taaffe admitted that the future of the Austro-Hungarian

Empire lay in keeping its subject nationalities in a balanced sense of mutual dissatisfaction.

13. "Balkanism" is not unlike Edward Said's "Orientalism," which is "a *distribution* of geopolitical awareness into aesthetic, scholarly, economic, sociological, historical and philological texts" and into the realm of ideas. Edward W. Said, *Orientalism* (New York: Vintage Books, 1979), 12.

14. Maria Todorova, *Imagining the Balkans* (Oxford: Oxford University Press, 1997), 118–19.

15. John Gunther, *Inside Europe* (New York: Harper, 1940), 437.

16. A Turkish word meaning "a chain of mountains," usually wooded, "Balkan" is a geographical term for the peninsula in southeastern Europe. Countries considered part of the Balkans include the former Yugoslavia (except Slovenia), Bulgaria, Romania, Albania, Greece, and Turkey, mainly because of its historical influence over the region. Around the beginning of the twentieth century, Europe had added to its glossary of *Schimpfwörter*, or disparagements, "Balkanization," which had come to denote the "parcelization of large and viable political units but had also become a synonym for a reversion to the tribal, the backward, the primitive, the barbarian" (Todorova 3). One can counter the equation of Balkanization with "parcelization" by pointing out that the unsettled period when the term acquired that connotation was, from one perspective, really a period of unification, consolidation, and even modernization as new political entities like Albania, Greece, Bulgaria, and the Kingdom of Serbs, Croats, and Slovenes were born. Only from the perspective of empires like Austria-Hungary should "parcelization" in the Balkan context be seen purely as a regressive negative.

The word first entered European consciousness because of terrorist groups like the International Macedonian Revolutionary Organization, the massacre of the Serbian king Alexander Obrenović and his wife, Draga, in 1903, the Balkan Wars of 1912–1913, and of course the assassination in 1914, but what remains today isn't historically particular; instead, Westerners have a more general repulsion for uncivilized savagery attributed to the whole region and its people. The Yugoslav wars of the 1990s just entrenched this attitude.

1 + THE KRAJINA

1. This wasn't the first time ethnic conflict had erupted in the Krajina. As far back as the sixteenth century, the rebellion of Orthodox Slavs under Austrian or Croatian control was suppressed violently. At the end of the First World War, some Croatian rioters burned the shops of Serbs who supported the unification of Serbs, Croats, and Slovenes. The Croats saw their hurried

inclusion in this state, which was controlled by a Serbian dynasty, as a continuation of the old order and a decline in their social position.

2. Harry De Windt, *Through Savage Europe, Being the Narrative of a Journey Throughout the Balkan States and European Russia* (London: Collins' Clear-Type Press, 1907), 87–88.

3. The Muslims were originally indigenous Slavs who converted to Islam after the Ottoman conquest in 1463. In Princip's time, according to the last Austro-Hungarian census in 1910, the ethnic breakdown in Bosnia-Herzegovina was as follows: 43.5 per cent Orthodox, 32.2 per cent Muslim, 23.3 per cent Catholic. In the last Yugoslav census of 1981, the numbers had changed to 44 per cent Muslim, 33 per cent Serb, 17 per cent Croat. In 2004 the U.S. State Department emended these numbers to 48.3 per cent Bosniak (Muslim), 34 per cent Serb, 15.4 per cent Croat.

4. Abdić's activities were probably as self-serving as they were magnanimous. Before the Yugoslav Wars, he was director of Agrokomerc, a state-affiliated food distribution company based in Velika Kladuša, one of the biggest companies in the Balkans. In 1988, it was learned that Agrokomerc had taken advantage of Yugoslavia's bank bond system, whose financial institutions were intertwined with the businesses to which they loaned money, and had issued over $300 million worth of promissory notes without backing. He was convicted by Yugoslav authorities but acquitted on appeal and hailed as a local hero. The story of Fikret Abdić winds down with the warrant for his arrest issued by Austrian police because of misuse of $8 million worth of funds, which Bosnian guest workers in Austria had collected for refugees in the Cazinska Krajina. He was charged with war crimes by the Bosnian government, though by that time he'd been granted political asylum and citizenship by the Croatian government of Franjo Tudjman, which refused to extradite him on constitutional grounds. After Tudjman's death, authorities in the new Croatia tried him on charges of war crimes in the Bihać pocket, and sentenced him to twenty years imprisonment (later reduced to fifteen). Misha Glenny, "The Godfather of Bihac," *The New York Review of Books* (August 12, 1993). www.nybooks.com/articles/2482 (accessed May 5, 2006).

5. Glenny, "The Godfather of Bihac."

6. Misha Glenny points out that there were Orthodox in the Krajina before the invited settling by the Habsbugs. But the migration led by Arsenije III established the territorial problems between Serbs and Croats that still exist today. Misha Glenny, *The Fall of Yugoslavia: The Third Balkan War* (New York: Penguin, 1996), 5.

7. In Dedijer, 30. Possibly he'd also been called *il principe bosniaco* by Italians in Venetian-held Dalmatia, and the name and Italian spelling had stuck. Since

Italian names and titles retained their spelling in Serbo-Croatian documents of the time, Dedijer concludes, the South Slavs would have pronounced the "c" of "Princip" "ts" not "ch" as it would be in Italian: "Printsip."

8. Glenny, *The Fall of Yugoslavia*, 3.

9. Under the Ottomans in the nineteenth century, peasants were heavily taxed. For example, there were taxes on houses, land, cattle, flowers, and beehives; each Christian family had to pay a tax for each male in the family (regardless of age) in place of serving in the Turkish army. In a speech published the day after the assassination in the *New York Times*, Serb-American physicist at Columbia University, Michael I. Pupin, said that the situation had actually worsened after Austria's takeover in 1878. People before had been allowed some liberty with the land. "Now an old woman cannot go into the forests and gather up an apronful of sticks for her fire without making herself liable to arrest and heavy punishment. No: the wood is first shipped to Vienna and then brought back to Bosnia and sold to the peasant at ten to fifteen times the price it should bring."

10. Princip, *The Sarajevo Trial, Volume I*, 68. That said, Princip didn't know or admit that the Austrians introduced some reforms to agrarian life: proper tax assessors, a land registry to prevent corruption by Muslim landlords, and a tithe-averaging system by which tithes were calculated on an average over the past ten years' harvest, so that a peasant whose production was increasing would pay less than the tithe on his current crop. Also, serfs were allowed to free themselves by paying an indemnity (which was introduced into Turkish law in 1876). In general, though, the feudal system remained in place. In 1914 roughly 93,368 serf families were working on *agaluk* states, about a third of all arable land. See Noel Malcolm, *Bosnia: A Short History* (Washington Square, NY: New York University Press, 1996), 140–41.

11. In Dedijer, *The Road to Sarajevo*, 189.

12. In Dedijer, *The Road to Sarajevo*, 189.

13. Martin Pappenheim, "Dr. Pappenhein's Conversations with Gavrilo Princip," ed. and trans. Hamilton Fish Armstrong, *Current History* (August 1927): 702.

14. In Dedijer, *The Road to Sarajevo*, 187.

15. In Dedijer, *The Road to Sarajevo*, 190.

16. I was later told the peak is called Mount Šator.

2 + THE KRAJINA, TRAVNIK, SARAJEVO

1. Božidar Tomić, "Poreklo i detinjstvo Gavrila Principa," *Nova Evropa* (October 26, 1939); my translation.

2. In Dedijer, *The Road to Sarajevo*, 194–95.

3. Stavrianos, *The Balkans Since 1453*, 464.

4. Pappenheim, "Conversations with Princip," 702.

5. Princip, *The Sarajevo Trial, Volume II*, 347–48.

6. Dedijer, *The Road to Sarajevo*, 194.

7. Dedijer, *The Road to Sarajevo*, 175.

8. The Bogomils were a Bulgarian heretical movement founded in the tenth century by a priest called "Bogumil" (beloved by God), which spread in the centuries that followed into Constantinople and parts of the Balkans. Among other things, Bogomils followed a dualist, Manichean theology based on the belief that life was a perpetual struggle between the principles of good and evil; they rejected the authority of any church on Earth, saw the cross as a hated symbol of false belief, and wore ascetic in their daily living (fasting long, abstaining from meat, liquor, marriage, and sex). They were also contemptuous of the Hebrew Bible, saying it was inspired by Satanel (the "el" apparently signifying divinity). Exceptions were the Psalms, the sixteen prophets, the Acts of the Apostles from the New Testament, the Epistles, and the Apocalypse.

9. The reason Cuvaj became a target was his handling of the victory of a Croat-Serb coalition in the Croatian *Sabor* (Parliament) in elections on December 11, 1911. In January the newly appointed *ban* promptly adjourned the *Sabor*, established a non-constitutional regime, and banned political gatherings.

10. In Dedijer, *The Road to Sarajevo*, 265.

11. On October 31, 1912, Ivan Planinščak shot at *ban* Cuvaj of Croatia, missed, and committed suicide. Croat Stjepan Dojčić returned from the United States, where he worked in a car factory in Chenoa, Illinois, shot and wounded the next *ban*, Baron Ivo Skerletz.

12. Cited in R.W. Seton-Watson, *Sarajevo: A Study in the Origins of the Great War* (London: Hutchinson and Co., 1926), 70.

13. According to Dedijer and other sources. In Martin Pappenheim's steno-graphic notes of his interviews with Princip, Princip says he went to Belgrade in 1911.

14. Pappenheim, "Conversations with Princip," 702.

15. Pappenheim, "Conversations with Princip," 702.

16. Princip, *The Sarajevo Trial, Volume II*, 350.

17. Princip, *The Sarajevo Trial, Volume I*, 16.

18. Princip, *The Sarajevo Trial, Volume II*, 336.

19. Princip, *The Sarajevo Trial, Volume I*, 32–33.

20. Edith Durham, *The Sarajevo Crime* (London: George Allen & Unwin, Ltd., 1925), 77.

21. Princip, *The Sarajevo Trial, Volume I*, 43; my translation.

22. De Windt, *Through Savage Europe*, 84.

23. Pappenheim, "Conversations with Princip," n.14.

24. Malcolm, *Bosnia: A Short History*, 144.

25. Malcolm, *Bosnia: A Short History*, 131.

3 ✦ BELGRADE

1. Wayne S. Vucinich, "Some Aspects of the Ottoman Legacy," *The Balkans in Transition: Essays on the Development of Balkan Life and Politics Since the Eighteenth Century*, Charles and Barbara Jelavich, eds. (Berkeley: University of California Press, 1963), 92–94. This was due to the interdict against wine in the Koran, which saw the rise of the coffee house as an institution. By 1914, of course, wine and spirits were available in cafés as well.

2. Vucinich, "Ottoman Legacy," 93–94.

3. Leon Trotsky, "Belgrade," *The War Correspondence of Leon Trotsky: The Balkan Wars 1912–13*, Brian Pearce, trans. George Weissman and Duncan Williams, eds. (New York: Monad Press, 1980), 62.

4. Vladimir Dedijer tells a slightly different story. He writes that Princip was promptly rejected at the Bosnian headquarters of the Serbian *komite*, which forced him to go in desperation to Prokopulje (197). Princip may have wanted to conceal his first rejection. Dedijer does not, however, cite a source for this part of the story. For the account of Tankosić's decision, he cites a lecture by N. Trišić in Sarajevo on November 10, 1940, as well as an article in *Politika*, June 30, 1914.

5. In Dedijer, *The Road to Sarajevo*, 197.

6. Princip, *The Sarajevo Trial, Volume I*, 18.

7. See note 2 in the Introduction.

8. Princip, *The Sarajevo Trial, Volume I*, 19.

9. According to Čabrinović's account at the trial, he made two return journeys to Sarajevo, one with books and one without (he had sent those by mail in a suitcase). On his first return, his mother "found several books and burned them, and the rest I read and gave to my most intimate friends to read" (*The Sarajevo Trial, Volume I*, 18). At his second return he made no mention of his mother opening the trunk, nor burning any books. Dedijer, however, conflates the two journeys. He also says Čabrinović's mother found the trunk with the anarchist books and "burned them all" (200).

10. Dedijer, *The Road to Sarajevo*, 200. Čabrinović didn't mention this second incident at the trial.

11. Princip, *The Sarajevo Trial, Volume I*, 21.

12. Princip, *The Sarajevo Trial, Volume I*, 90.

13. Pappenheim, "Conversations with Princip," 706.

14. Princip, *The Sarajevo Trial, Volume I*, 23–24.

15. Princip, *The Sarajevo Trial, Volume I*, 57.

16. Pappenheim, "Conversations with Princip," 705–06.

17. Princip, *The Sarajevo Trial, Volume I*, 24.

18. In David Mackenzie, *Apis, The Congenial Conspirator: The Life of Colonel Dragutin T. Dimitrijević* (Boulder, CO: East European Monographs, 1989), 136.

19. This story emerged in the context of Apis's 1917 show trial before a Serbian military tribunal in Salonika for allegedly conspiring to murder Serbian Crown Prince Alexander.

20. Rade Malobabić was a suspect in the Zagreb Treason Trials of 1909.

21. In Mackenzie, *Apis*, 130.

22. Mackenzie, *Apis*, 124–25.

23. Responsibility for his murder could lie with Milošević, who by 2000 had been ousted in a popular uprising, and who may have wanted to prevent the unappetizing possibility of Stambolić's political resurrection.

24. Before leaving the hotel the next morning I had a suspicion that the ISO setting on my manual camera didn't match the film I'd put in. This had happened a few years ago, and I'd fixed the problem by lowering the shutters on the windows, crouching inside the clothes' cabinet with the door nearly shut, and opening the camera back to see the film spool. I did so again, but discovered a few weeks later that too much light had entered the camera this time. The film was ruined. As it turned out, the camera was set at the right ISO. The photo of Belgrade is from an online source: http://ec.europa.eu/enlargement/press_corner/photo_gallery/serbia_en.htm (accessed September 30, 2009).

25. In Dedijer, *The Road to Sarajevo*, 297.

26. Princip, *The Sarajevo Trial, Volume I*, 236.

27. Cited in Joachim Remak, *Sarajevo: The Story of a Political Murder* (London: Weidenfeld and Nicolson, 1959), 82. Remak uses the French translation of the trial prepared by journalist (and Freemason) Alfred Mousset, *Un drame historique de l'attentat de Sarajevo. Documents inédits et texte intégral de sténogrammes du procès* (Paris: Payot, 1930). The less colourful translation of Mićo Mićić's comment, which comes from the so-called Belgrade copy of 1925, prepared by Vojislav Bogičević (which is the one cited throughout this book), is as follows: "I went back because there was some brandy left" (237).

28. Princip, *The Sarajevo Trial, Volume I*, 62.

29. Hans Koning, *Death of a Schoolboy* (London: Allison and Busby, 1974), 70–71.

4 + VIŠEGRAD, FOČA

1. The "convertible mark" refers to the Deutschemark, the currency to which the Bosnian currency was fixed at par. Since the replacement of the German mark by the euro in 2002, the convertible mark uses the same fixed exchange rate to euro that the Deutschemark has.

2. Some reports written during the war argued against the commonly held perception of Serb atrocities in Goražde. See for example Vaughn S. Forrest and Yossef Bodansky's "The Truth about Goražde," written on behalf of the Task Force on Terrorism and Unconventional Warfare, a House Republican Research Committee, May 4, 1994. www.srpska-mreza.com/bosnia/gorazde. html (accessed May 1, 2006). It is of course worth nothing that this article, which advocates against U.S. involvement in the Bosnian war, was written a full year before the Bosnian-Serb massacre of some 8,000 Muslim men and boys at Srebrenica. Had the U.S. acted decisively against the Serbs earlier, the conditions for the Srebrenica massacre might have been mitigated and the massacre itself possibly prevented.

3. Ivo Andrić, *The Pasha's Concubine and Other Tales*, trans. Joseph Hitrec (London: Allen & Unwin. 1969: Svjetlost, 1986), 13. The bridge on the Žepa was moved eight kilometres upstream in 1967, to save it from being destroyed by the storage lake for the Bajina Bašta hydroelectric plant. A report originally published in *Slobodna Bosna* described the problems with this and other old Bosnian bridges: "Already before the war a big crack had appeared on the bridge, which was then only partially repaired. Not long ago this crack widened and became a clear sign that the bridge—which is supposed soon to be proclaimed a Bosnian national monument—was in great danger....Changes in the water level threaten the bridge. In the postwar years the bridge was renovated (1949–52) and it was in excellent shape up until the construction of the Višegrad hydro-electric plant. The latter had a legal obligation to protect the bridge, but the conservation and restoration work was interrupted when the war broke out in 1992. For thirteen years already, the stone in the piles of the bridge has been subjected to erosion because of constant changes in the water level: when water is released from the hydro-electric plant, the piles are largely submerged; but when the level drops, the stone is exposed to the air. The changing level causes rapid weakening of the stone....A year ago [in 2003] the damage to the bridge at Višegrad became so extensive that the passage of motor vehicles across it was forbidden. However, only rare local inhabitants are really worried today about the fate of the bridge, and some of them even assert that the ban on traffic over the bridge has merely complicated their lives....The bridge over the Drina, a former tourist attraction, today attracts only a handful of curious visitors. A nearby souvenir kiosk offers Chinese souvenirs and a few amateur oil paintings with images of the bridge. In the town, which has a street, a school and a library bearing Andrić's name, neither his books nor monographs about the bridge are on sale!" Adisa Bašić, "The Slow Death of Bosnia's Bridges," *Bosnia Report*

41 (August–September 2004). www.bosnia.org.uk/bosrep/report_format. cfm?articleid=1123&reportid=165 (accessed May 10, 2006).

4. Paul Blanchard, *Blue Guide Yugoslavia* (London: A & C Black, 1989), 368.

5. These Muslims, however, did not likely live in Višegrad's town core. According to the Helsinki Committee for Human Rights in Bosnia and Herzegovina, in their "Report on the Status of Human Rights in Bosnia and Herzegovina (Analysis for the period January–December 2006)," there was only one Bosniak living there. www.bh-hchr.org/reports.htm (accessed May 10, 2006).

6. Ivo Andrić, *The Bridge on the Drina*, trans. Lovett F. Edwards (Chicago: University of Chicago Press, 1977), 16.

7. Andrei Simić debunks John Fine and Robert Donia's optimistic notion that Bosnia had a basic harmonious history of multiculturalism. He suggests instead that suspicion and hatred were really always central and always there. In the country, relations have never been that interconnected and harmonious. See "Nationalism as a Folk Ideology," *Neighbors at War: Anthropological Perspectives on Yugoslav Ethnicity, Culture, and History*, eds. Joel M. Halpern and David A. Kideckel (University Park, PA: Pennsylvania State University Press, 2000), 103–15.

8. Malcolm, *Bosnia: A Short History*, xxi.

9. For more on Ivo Andrić and the bridge in the context of the first days of the war, see Chandler Rosenberger, "Bridges on the Drina," Institute of Current World Affairs, July 8, 1993. http://people.bu.edu/crr/publications.html (accessed May 15, 2006).

10. Ivo Andrić, *Bosnian Chronicle* (New York: Knopf, 1963), 217.

11. In Dedijer, *The Road to Sarajevo*, 215.

12. Milan Lukić, along with his cousin, Sredoje, and their family friend, Mitar Vasiljević, was indicted by the War Crimes Tribunal in The Hague in 2001 for crimes against humanity and violations of the laws or customs of war. Among other crimes, he was alleged to have forced more than sixty Bosnian Muslim women, children, and elderly men into a house in Višegrad on June 14, 1992. The house was set on fire and those who tried to flee were shot. Among those murdered were seventeen children between the ages of two days and fourteen years. Milan Lukić was charged with committing a similar crime in the Višegrad area on June 27, 1992. In that case, he allegedly forced a group of seventy Bosnian Muslims inside a house, set it on fire, and burned them alive. Lukić was on the run for seven years, living in Bosnia and Serbia, where he was arrested three times for racketeering and other organized crimes, but released. In 2005 the Belgrade district court convicted him *in absentia* to twenty years' imprisonment for the 1992 kidnapping

and killing of sixteen Muslims in Sjeverin, Serbia. He was finally arrested in Argentina in August 2005. In 2007 the War Crimes Tribunal granted the prosecution's motion that his case be tried by the Bosnian State Court. For more, see Ed Vulliamy's reports in *The Guardian*, "Bloody Trail of Butchery at the Bridge" (March 11, 1996). www.usna.edu/Users/history/tucker/hh367/ ButcheryattheBridge.htm; and "The Warlord of Visegrad" [sic], *The Guardian*, (August 11, 2005). www.guardian.co.uk/world/2005/aug/11/warcrimes. features11 (accessed May 20, 2006).

13. John Allcock, *Explaining Yugoslavia*, (New York: Columbia University Press, 2000), 346. Allcock adds complexity to the concept of Yugoslavia by focusing on conceptualization of space. He says that the "symbolic freight of space (that which is actually signified by references to space in their relation to national identity) is intimately woven with a people's consciousness of history. Spaces are significant spaces, and the significances with which they are endowed are to be understood in terms of the historical narratives which link people to territory or places" (338). He mentions links made between contemporary nation states and medieval empires. The various parts of the former Yugoslavia, he writes, "offer a superb range of different ways of conceptualising symbolically the spaces within which they see themselves as belonging and in relation to which they have come to define themselves over time" (339).

14. The Catholic Church in Bosnia-Herzegovina, Croatia, and Slovenia also interpreted "Yugoslavism" as a form of Serbian nationalism. In August 1914, the Archbishop of Zagreb called the war against the Serbs a holy war, and similar statements by Bosnian Archbishop Stadler and Bishop of Mostar Monsignor Mišić emphasized the perceived Greek Orthodox threat. As one historian noted, it was in Catholic Slovenia that "there appeared the famous slogan "(Hang) Serbs on willows" ("*Srbe na vrbe*"). See Dušan Bataković's "The Balkan Piedmont Serbia and the Yugoslav Question." www.rastko.rs/ istorija/batakovic/batakovic-piedmont_eng.html (accessed May 22, 2006).

15. Vaso Čubrilović was one of the Serbs behind the shrill "Memorandum of the Serbian Academy of Arts and Sciences" in 1986, which drew attention to alleged abuses against Serbs by the Albanians in Kosovo. Čubrilović also served as an advisor to the Royal Yugoslav government after the First World War, when he wrote the official government memorandum "The Expulsion of the Albanians." He advocated the need for an "emigration psychosis" through a government-run programme of persecution that would drive the Albanians out to Turkey or Albania. Čubrilović went on to hold various ministerial posts in Tito's government, and was Tito's first minister of Agriculture. See Philip J. Cohen, "The Complicity of Serbian Intellectuals

in Genocide in the 1990s" in *This Time We Knew: Western Responses to Genocide in Bosnia*, eds. Thomas Cushman and Stjepan G. Meštrović (New York: New York University Press, 1996), 40. In Yugoslav parlance, "the term 'ethnically clean' emerged after 1981 in Kosovo with the accusation, by federal and Serbian authorities, of an alleged plan of Kosovo Albanians to create a Serb-free Kosovo." Rajko Muršić, "The Yugoslav Dark Side of Humanity" in *Neighbors at War: Anthropological Perspectives on Yugoslav Ethnicity, Culture, and History*, eds. Joel M. Halpern and David A. Kideckel (University Park, PA: Pennsylvania State University Press, 2000), 58, n.4.

16. The Serbs renamed the town "Srbinje," but all the signs read "Foča."

17. Tim Clancy, *Bosnia & Herzegovina: The Bradt Travel Guide* (Guilford, CT: The Globe Pequot Press Inc., 2004), 161.

18. Andrej Gustinčić, Reuters, in Ed Vulliamy, *Seasons in Hell: Understanding Bosnia's War* (New York: St. Martin's Press, 1994), 90–91.

19. Former Bosnian-Serb leader and indicted war criminal Radovan Karadžić was eventually arrested in Serbia in 2008. While still in Bosnia, he was known to have hidden in Čelebići. According to a report in *The Guardian*, U.S. and German peacekeeping forces raided his hideout in March 2002, only to find him already gone. The American military blamed an unnamed French soldier for sabotaging the mission by leaking it to one of Karadžić's bodyguards, a charge denied by the French government, which noted that there was no evidence for the charge (corroborated by the British, though they do confirm that a telephone message in Serbo-Croatian alerting the Bosnian Serbs was intercepted). For the full report, see Richard Norton Taylor and Jon Henley's "US falsely blamed French soldier for Karadzic escape" (March 9, 2002). www.guardian.co.uk/world/2002/mar/09/balkans.warcrimes (accessed June 20, 2006). See also Jonathan Steele, Richard Norton-Taylor, and Maggie O'Kane's report in *The Guardian* for further examples of French inertia when it comes to arresting war criminals like Karadžić, "Raid to net prime suspect botched by Nato" (March 1, 2002). www.guardian.co.uk/world/2002/mar/01/warcrimes.richardnortontaylor (accessed June 20, 2006).

5 ✦ DOBOJ, TUZLA

1. Princip, *The Sarajevo Trial, Volume I*, 63.

2. Princip, *The Sarajevo Trial, Volume I*, 170.

3. Princip, *The Sarajevo Trial, Volume I*, 82.

4. At the trial, Princip was careful to note that one of Mitar's sons, Jovo, didn't see the weapons at all. He thereby convinced the authorities of Jovo's lack of involvement.

5. In Remak, *Sarajevo: The Story of a Political Murder*, 86.

6.   Dedijer, *The Road to Sarajevo*, 299.

7.   Dedijer, *The Road to Sarajevo*, 299.

8.   Princip, *The Sarajevo Trial, Volume I*, 111.

9.   Princip, *The Sarajevo Trial, Volume I*, 182.

10. Princip, *The Sarajevo Trial, Volume I*, 182.

11. Princip, *The Sarajevo Trial, Volume I*, 192.

12. Princip, *The Sarajevo Trial, Volume I*, 40.

13. At the trial, Princip said the following: "We decided that one of us would go. Because I had already gone once we [Princip and Ilić] decided that he should go." Princip, *The Sarajevo Trial, Volume I*, 66.

14. Mak Dizdar's poem on a monument commemorating the massacre reads as follows:

    HERE ONE DOES NOT LIVE JUST

    TO LIVE

    HERE ONE DOES NOT LIVE JUST

    TO DIE

    HERE ONE ALSO DIES

    TO LIVE

An inscription after the poem explains that "Serbian fascist aggressors" killed seventy-one young people.

6 ✦ HERZEGOVINA

1.   Paul Blanchard, *Blue Guide Yugoslavia* (London: A & C Black, 1989), 365.

2.   De Windt, *Through Savage Europe*, 91–92.

3.   Dedijer, *The Road to Sarajevo*, 176.

4.   Michael I. Pupin, "Austria to Blame, Says Prof. Pupin," *New York Times* (June 29, 1914): 1.

5.   In Dedijer, *The Road to Sarajevo*, 283.

6.   Princip, *The Sarajevo Trial, Volume I*, 116.

7.   Steven L. Burg and Paul S. Shoup, *The War in Bosnia-Herzegovina: Ethnic Conflict and International Intervention* (Armonk, NY: M.E. Sharpe, 2000), 19.

8.   Burg and Shoup, *The War in Bosnia-Herzegovina*, 20.

9.   Misha Glenny, *The Fall of Yugoslavia: The Third Balkan War* (London: Penguin, 1996), 157.

10. John V.A. Fine Jr., *The Late Medieval Balkans: A Critical Survey from the Late Twelfth Century to the Ottoman Conquest* (Ann Arbor: University of Michigan Press, 1987), 486. See also Fine's *The Bosnian Church: A New Interpretation, A study of the Bosnian Church and Its Place in State and Society from the 13th to the 15th Centuries* (Boulder, CO:

East European Monographs, 1975). Also, for an overview of the relationship between the *stećci* and the Bosnian Church, see Noel Malcolm's *Bosnia: A Short History* (Washington Square, NY: New York University Press, 1996), 29–31.

11. The Arslanagić Bridge, built in 1574 by Vizier Mehmed-Paša Sokolović, and which was moved closer to Trebinje because of damage from the hydroelctric dam, was a notable structured spared.

7 ✦ SARAJEVO II

1. Princip, *The Sarajevo Trial, Volume I*, 147.
2. Princip, *The Sarajevo Trial, Volume II*, 337.
3. Princip, *The Sarajevo Trial, Volume I*, 147.
4. In Dedijer, *The Road to Sarajevo*, 315.
5. In Dedijer, *The Road to Sarajevo*, 306.
6. Princip, *The Sarajevo Trial, Volume I*, 120.
7. One argument for Ilić's seeming indifference about the possibilities of the second troika's success was his interest in making the conspiracy appear to be a strictly local affair, thereby concealing Belgrade's role. The Austrian authorities, however, would have dismissed this possibility, using the assassination as a pretext for an attack on Serbia proper.
8. Princip, *The Sarajevo Trial, Volume 1*, 120.
9. Princip, *The Sarajevo Trial, Volume 1*, 123.
10. On this point I follow Dedijer's information, taken from Serbian historian Slobodan Janković, who in turn cited Black Hand Central Committee member Čeda Popović. The English translation of *The Sarajevo Trial* repeatedly names Brod as the site of Ilić's unexplained trip.
11. See Dedijer, *The Road to Sarajevo*, 394.
12. Princip, *The Sarajevo Trial, Volume 1*, 152.
13. Numerous reports suggest that Serbian Prime Minister Pašić had learned of the plot and tried to warn the authorities in Vienna, but unofficially so as to avoid the charge of Serbian complicity and inaction. Pašić denied the report. In the *Neues Wiener Tageblatt* (June 28, 1914), Jovanović-Pižon said he warned Bilinski that "among the Serb youths there might be one who will put a ball cartridge in his rifle and he may fire it." See Dedijer, n.103, 507. The *New York Times* quoted the following dispatch from the *London Daily Mail* on June 29, 1914: "Before the Archduke went to Bosnia last Wednesday, the Serbian Minister here expressed doubts as to the wisdom of the journey, saying the country was in a very turbulent condition and the Serbian part of the population might organize a demonstration against the Archduke. The Minister said if the Archduke went himself he certainly ought to leave his wife at

home, because Bosnia was no place for a woman in its present disturbed state. The Minister's words proved correct."

14. In *Sarajevski Atentat*, author Borivoje Jevtić says Princip told his acquaintances at Semiz's wine shop about the chance meeting and said he couldn't shoot because a policeman was directly behind him. A Bosnian government official reported that at Princip's first interrogation on June 28, 1914, he said he didn't want to fire his pistol in the shop for fear of hitting the duchess. But the official transcripts of the interrogation show no evidence for this meeting on June 25. Dedijer, *The Road to Sarajevo*, 312.

15. On the "Turkish" side an "Ottoman nobility led an army composed not only of Muslims but also contingents from other European groups who were their vassals—including other Slavs, among whom were Serbs." John B. Allcock, *Explaining Yugoslavia* (New York: Columbia University Press, 2000), 315. According to Georges Castellan, "What is clear is that Murad's army was reinforced by contingents from his vassals: Prince Constantine of Velbužd a Bulgarian, Marko Kraljević a Serbian and enemy of Lazarus but also Muslim vassal Emirs and allies from Asia Minor. Basileus John V was missing as he was no longer able to muster sufficient troops. Against these were drawn the armies of Lazarus and King Tvrtko which were reinforced by Wallachian contingents from the Voevod Mircea and Albanians under George Balsha and Demeter Jonima." In Allcock, *Explaining Yugoslavia*, 316.

16. In Thomas Emmert, "The Battle of Kosovo: Early Reports of Victory and Defeat" in Wayne S. Vucinich and Thomas A. Emmert, eds., *Kosovo: The Legacy of a Medieval Battle* (Minneapolis: University of Minnesota Press, 1991), 24.

17. Tim Judah, *The Serbs: History, Myth and the Destruction of Yugoslavia* (New Haven, CT: Yale University Press, 1997), 30.

18. His other sister, Vukosava, was studying at a teacher's college in Karlovac.

19. Princip, *The Sarajevo Trial, Volume I*, 105.

20. Dedijer, *The Road to Sarajevo*, 319; my emphasis.

21. In Remak, *Sarajevo: The Story of a Political Murder*, 130.

22. In Dedijer, *The Road to Sarajevo*, 13.

23. In Dedijer, *The Road to Sarajevo*, 13.

24. There is film footage of this moment online at www.firstworldwar.com/video/ferdinand.htm.

25. In Dedijer, *The Road to Sarajevo*, 14.

26. In Remak, *Sarajevo: The Story of a Political Murder*, 137.

27. Pappenheim, "Conversations with Princip," 706.

28. In Dedijer, *The Road to Sarajevo*, 321.

29. Count Harrach's testimony is available in Princip, *The Sarajevo Trial, Volume II*, 326.

30. A photograph of the bas-relief is available in Dedijer's Serbo-Croatian version of *The Road to Sarajevo*, titled *Sarajevo 1914* (Beograd: Prosveta, 1966).

31. The gun used by Princip (serial no. 19074) was found in a Jesuit community house in Styria, Austria, in 2004. The Jesuit priest who administered the last rites to the archduke and his wife, Father Anton Puntigam, was entrusted with the weapon, as well as the other pistols and percussion bombs, by the Bosnian ministry in Vienna. He had declared his intentions of opening a museum to commemorate the archduke but was prevented from doing so by the war. When he died in 1926, the objects were offered to the archduke's family, who declined to take them. The objects were put on display at the Vienna Museum of Military History in June 2004.

32. In Dedijer, *The Road to Sarajevo*, 197.

33. The line along the top of the plaque is from a poem titled "The Mountain Wreath" by Montenegrin Prince-Bishop and poet Petar Petrović-Njegoš. It reads: "Blessed is he whose name live forever, a good reason had he to be alive." The poem, a staple for schoolchildren in the former Yugoslavia, concerns in part the need to solve the "problem" in Montenegro of converts to Islam. Its place on the plaque lends support to the notion that many Serbs considered the assassins Serbian nationalists first and foremost. The next line on the plaque is "St. Vitus' Day's Heroes." The names in the lefthand column are Nedeljko Čabrinović, Veljko Čubrilović, Nedjo Kerović. In the middle: Gavrilo Princip, Danilo Ilić, Mihajlo Miško Jovanović, Jakov Milović, Bogdan Žerajić. On the right: Trifko Grabež, Mitar Kerović, Marko Perin. Translated by Teodora Hictaler Fabijančić.

8 ✦ THERESIENSTADT

1. Leo Pfeffer, *Istraga u Sarajevskom atentatu* (Zagreb: Nova Evropa, 1938), 29. My translation, following Dedijer.

2. Lavender Cassels, *The Archduke and the Assassin: Sarajevo, June 28th 1914* (London: F. Muller, 1984), 156.

3. Princip, *The Sarajevo Trial, Volume I*, 45.

4. Princip, *The Sarajevo Trial, Volume II*, 439. Ilić would have been arrested in any case once Princip's police registration was noticed.

5. Princip, *The Sarajevo Trial, Volume II*, 506–07.

6. Dedijer, *The Road to Sarajevo*, 332

7. Princip, *The Sarajevo Trial, Volume II*, 353.

8. The Black Hand was mentioned only once in the trial, in a question directed to Čabrinović by the state prosecutor. Čabrinović said he had heard of it and knew it existed in officers' circles but otherwise claimed ignorance about it.

9. Princip, *The Sarajevo Trial, Volume I*, 22.

10. Princip, *The Sarajevo Trial, Volume I*, 68.
11. Princip, *The Sarajevo Trial, Volume I*, 68.
12. Allcock, *Explaining Yugoslavia*, 327.
13. Princip, *The Sarajevo Trial, Volume I*, 119.
14. Princip, *The Sarajevo Trial, Volume I*, 122,123, 131.
15. Princip, *The Sarajevo Trial, Volume II*, 539, n.76.
16. Princip, *The Sarajevo Trial, Volume I*, 121.
17. *Spomenica Danila Ilića* (Sarajevo: Štamparija Petra N. Čakovića, 1922), 76; 77. Original translation: Teodora Hictaler Fabijančić.
18. Princip, *The Sarajevo Trial, Volume II*, 525.
19. Princip, *The Sarajevo Trial, Volume II*, 525.
20. Princip's birth date was in dispute at the trial. The parish register recorded the date as July 13, 1894, but the civil register, also kept by the parish, recorded it as June 13, 1894. If Princip were twenty years of age at the time of the assassination, he would have been condemned to death under Austro-Hungarian law. Ultimately the court decided to believe Princip's mother's testimony that he was born on July 13.
21. Princip, *The Sarajevo Trial, Volume II*, 527.
22. Following the recommendation of the Minister of Finance responsible for Bosnia-Herzegovina, Dr. Leon von Bilinski, the emperor commuted the death sentences of Nedjo Kerović and Jakov Milović to penal servitude for twenty years and life respectively. Among the accused who paid the heaviest price was Lazar Djukić, the student who declined Ilić's invitation to participate in the assassination but led him to the other young Sarajevans of the second troika. He got ten years imprisonment, a sentence that was increased (like that of Čubrilović, Popović, Kranjčević, and others, who were tried in 1915 for their involvement in Young Bosnian secret societies). He went mad from starvation in Theresienstadt and died in Prague on March 19, 1917. His remains were never found. For the full verdict see Princip, *The Sarajevo Trial, Volume II*, 527–30.
23. Of the 141,000 prisoners in Theresienstadt between 1941 and 1945, 35,000 died in the ghetto and 88,000 were shipped to concentration camps in the east, such as Auschwitz.
24. A German phrase, "Arbeit macht frei" literally means "work makes (one) free." Other translations include "work brings freedom," "work shall set you free/will free you," or "work liberates."
25. Based on Franz Werfel's memories of a meeting with Čabrinović in Theresienstadt, described in a 1917 issue of *Die Neue Rundschau* of Berlin, the cell was lit by an "unnatural yellow luminescence." In Pappenheim, "Conversations with Princip," 701.

26. In Dedijer, *The Road to Sarajevo*, 354.
27. Pappenheim, "Conversations with Princip," 702.
28. Pappenheim, "Conversations with Princip," 702.
29. Pappenheim, "Conversations with Princip," 703.
30. Pappenheim, "Conversations with Princip," 703.
31. Pappenheim, "Conversations with Princip," 705.
32. Pappenheim, "Conversations with Princip," 705.
33. Pappenheim, "Conversations with Princip," 706.
34. This according to the man responsible for transporting Princip's remains to Sarajevo. Quoted from Nikola Trišić, *Sarajevski atentat u Svjetlu Bibliografskih Podataka* (Belgrade: Veselin Masleša, 1960), 89.

CONCLUSION

1. "Letter to Vaso Čubrilović's Daughter." *Assassination at Sarajevo: The Event which Sparked off the First World War* (London: Jackdaw Publications, 1966), no. 4. Original translation: Teodora Hictaler Fabijančić.

✦ BIBLIOGRAPHY

Allcock, John B. *Explaining Yugoslavia*. New York: Columbia University Press, 2000.

Andrić, Ivo. *Bosnian Chronicle*. Joseph Hitrec, trans. New York: Knopf, 1963.

Andrić, Ivo. *The Pasha's Concubine and Other Tales*. Joseph Hitrec, trans. London: George Allen & Unwin, 1969.

Bašić, Adisa. "The Slow Death of Bosnia's Bridges." *Bosnia Report* 41 (August–September 2004): www.bosnia.org.uk/bosrep/report_format. cfm?articleid=1123&reportid=165 (accessed May 10, 2006).

Bataković, Dušan. "The Balkan Piedmont Serbia and the Yugoslav Question." www.rastko.rs/istorija/batakovic/batakovic-piedmont_eng.html (accessed May 22, 2006).

Berg, Steven L. and Paul S. Shoup. *The War in Bosnia-Herzegovina: Ethnic Conflict and International Intervention*. Armonk, NY: M.E. Sharpe, 2000.

Blanchard, Paul. *Blue Guide Yugoslavia*. London: A & C Black, 1989.

Cassels, Lavender. *The Archduke and the Assassin: Sarajevo, June 28th 1914*. London: F. Muller, 1984.

Clancy, Tim. *Bosnia & Herzegovina: The Bradt Travel Guide*. Guilford, CT: The Globe Pequot Press Inc., 2004.

Cohen, Philip J. "The Complicity of Serbian Intellectuals in Genocide in the 1990s." *This Time We Knew: Western Responses to Genocide in Bosnia*. Thomas Cushman and Stjepan G. Meštrović, eds. New York: New York University Press, 1996. 39–64.

Čubrilović, Veljko. "Letter to Daughter." *Assassination at Sarajevo: The Event which Sparked Off the First World War*. London: Jackdaw Publications, 1966. No. 4.

Dedijer, Vladimir. *Sarajevo 1914*. Beograd: Prosveta, 1966.

Dedijer, Vladimir. *The Road to Sarajevo*. New York: Simon and Schuster, 1966.

De Windt, Harry. *Through Savage Europe, Being the Narrative of a Journey Throughout the Balkan States and European Russia*. London: Collins' Clear-Type Press, 1907.

Donia, Robert J. and John V.A. Fine Jr. *Bosnia and Hercegovina: A Tradition Betrayed*. London: Hurst and Company, 1994.

Durham, Edith. *The Serajevo Crime*. London: George Allen & Unwin, Ltd., 1925.

Durham, Edith. *Twenty Years of Balkan Tangle*. London: George Allen & Unwin, 1920.

Emmert, Thomas. "The Battle of Kosovo: Early Reports of Victory and Defeat." *Kosovo: The Legacy of a Medieval Battle*. Wayne S. Vucinich and Thomas A. Emmert, eds. Minneapolis: University of Minnesota Press, 1991.

Eterovich, Francis H. and Christopher Spalatin, eds. *Croatia: Land, People, Culture, Volume I*. Toronto: University of Toronto Press, 1970.

Fine, John V.A. Jr. *The Bosnian Church: A New Interpretation, A study of the Bosnian Church and Its Place in State and Society from the 13th to the 15th Centuries*. Boulder, CO: East European Monographs, 1975.

Fine, John V.A. Jr. *The Late Medieval Balkans: A Critical Survey from the Late Twelfth Century to the Ottoman Conquest*. Ann Arbor: University of Michigan Press, 1987.

Forrest, Vaugh S. and Yossef Bodansky. "The Truth about Goražde." *The Task Force on Terrorism and Unconventional Warfare, a House Republican Research Committee* (May 4, 1994):www.srpska-mreza.com/bosnia/gorazde.html (accessed May 1, 2006).

Glenny, Misha. *The Balkans: Nationalism, War and the Great Powers 1804–1999*. New York: Viking, 1999.

Glenny, Misha. *The Fall of Yugoslavia: The Third Balkan War*. London: Penguin, 1996.

Glenny, Misha. "The Godfather of Bihac," *The New York Review of Books* (August 12, 1993): www.nybooks.com/articles/2482 (accessed May 5, 2006).

Glenny, Misha. "Why the Balkans Are So Violent." Rev. of *Love Thy Neighbor: A Story of War*, by Peter Maas. *The New York Review of Books* (September 19, 1996): www.nybooks.com/articles/1426 (accessed May 5, 2006).

Grandits, Hannes and Christian Promitzer. "Former Comrades at War: Historical Perspectives on Ethnic Cleansing in Croatia." *Neighbors at War: Anthropological Perspectives on Yugoslav Ethnicity, Culture, and History*. Joel M. Halpern and David A. Kideckel, eds. University Park, PA: Pennsylvania State University Press, 2000. 125–42.

Gunther, John. *Inside Europe*. New York: Harper, 1940.

Hammel, E.A. "Lessons from the Yugoslav Labyrinth." *Neighbors at War: Anthropological Perspectives on Yugoslav Ethnicity, Culture, and History*. Joel M. Halpern and David A. Kideckel, eds. University Park, PA: Pennsylvania State University Press, 2000. 19–38.

Helsinki Committee for Human Rights in Bosnia and Herzegovina. "Report on the Status of Human Rights in Bosnia and Herzegovina (Analysis for the period January–December 2006)." www.bh-hchr.org/reports.htm (accessed May 10, 2006).

Jelavich, Barabara. *History of the Balkans, Twentieth Century, Volume II*. Cambridge: Cambridge University Press, 1983.

Jevtić, Borivoje. *Sarajevski Atentat: Sećanja i Utisci*. Sarajevo: Štamparija Petra N. Đakovića, 1924.

Judah, Tim. *The Serbs: History, Myth and the Destruction of Yugoslavia*. New Haven, CT: Yale University Press, 1997.

Koning, Hans. *Death of a Schoolboy*. London: Allison and Busby, 1974.

Mackenzie, David. *Apis, The Congenial Conspirator: The Life of Colonel Dragutin T. Dimitrijević*. Boulder, CO: East European Monographs, 1989.

Mackenzie, David. *The "Black Hand" on Trial, Salonika, 1917*. Boulder, CO: East European Monographs, 1995.

Malcolm, Noel. *Bosnia: A Short History*. Washington Square, NY: New York University Press, 1996.

Muršič, Rajko. "The Yugoslav Dark Side of Humanity." *Neighbors at War: Anthropological Perspectives on Yugoslav Ethnicity, Culture, and History*. Joel M. Halpern and David A. Kideckel, eds. University Park, PA: Pennsylvania State University Press, 2000. 56–77.

New York Times (June 29, 1914): 1–5.

Norris, David A. *In the Wake of the Balkan Myth: Questions of Identity and Modernity*. New York: St. Martin's Press, 1999.

Pappenheim, Martin. "Dr. Pappenheim's Conversations with Princip." Hamilton Fish Armstrong, ed. and trans. *Current History* (August 1927): 699–707.

Petrovic, Edit. "Ethnonationalism and the Dissolution of Yugoslavia." *Neighbors at War: Anthropological Perspectives on Yugoslav Ethnicity, Culture, and History*. Joel M. Halpern and David A. Kideckel, eds. University Park, PA: Pennsylvania State University Press, 2000. 164–76.

Pfeffer, Leo. *Istraga u Sarajevskom atentatu*. Zagreb: Nova Evropa, 1938.

Princip, Gavrilo. *The Sarajevo Trial, Volumes I and II*. W.A. Dolph Owings, intro. W.A. Dolph Owings, Elizabeth Pribic, and Nikola Pribic, trans. Chapel Hill, NC: Documentary Publications, 1984.

Pupin, Michael I. "Austria to Blame, Says Prof. Pupin." *New York Times* (June 29, 1914): 1.

Remak, Joachim. *Sarajevo: The Story of a Political Murder*. London: Weidenfeld and Nicolson, 1959.

Rosenberger, Chandler. "Bridges on the Drina." *Institute of Current World Affairs* (July 8, 1993): http://people.bu.edu/crr/publications.html (accessed May 15, 2006).

Seton-Watson, R.W. *Sarajevo: A Study in the Origins of the Great War*. London: Hutchinson and Co., 1926.

Simić, Andrei. "Nationalism as a Folk Ideology," *Neighbors at War: Anthropological Perspectives on Yugoslav Ethnicity, Culture, and History*. Joel M. Halpern and David A. Kideckel, eds. University Park, PA: Pennsylvania State University Press, 2000. 103–15.

Spomenica Danila Ilića. Sarajevo: Štamparija Petra N. Đakovića, 1922.

Stavrianos, L.S. *The Balkans Since 1453*. New York: Rinehart, 1961.

Steele, Jonathan, Richard Norton-Taylor, and Maggie O'Kane. "Raid to net prime suspect botched by Nato." *The Guardian* (March 1, 2002): www.guardian.co.uk/world/2002/mar/01/warcrimes.richardnortontaylor (accessed June 20, 2006).

Taylor, Richard Norton and Jon Henley. "US falsely blamed French soldier for Karadzic escape" (March 9, 2002): www.guardian.co.uk/world/2002/mar/09/balkans.warcrimes (accessed June 20, 2006).

Todorova, Maria. *Imagining the Balkans*. Oxford: Oxford University Press, 1997.

Tomić, Božidar. "Poreklo i Detinjstvo Gavrila Principa." *Nova Evropa* (October 26, 1939).

Trišić, Nikola. *Sarajevski Atentat u Svjetlu Bibliografskih Podataka*. Belgrade: Veselin Masleša, 1960.

Trotsky, Leon. "Belgrade." *The War Correspondence of Leon Trotsky: The Balkan Wars 1912–13*. Brian Pearce, trans. George Weissman and Duncan Williams, eds. New York: Monad Press, 1980: 61–64.

Vucinich, Wayne S. "Some Aspects of the Ottoman Legacy." *The Balkans in Transition: Essays on the Development of Balkan Life and Politics Since the Eighteenth Century*. Charles and Barbara Jelavich, eds. Berkeley: University of California Press, 1963. 92–94.

Vulliamy, Ed. "Bloody Trail of Butchery at the Bridge." *The Guardian* (March 11, 1996): www.usna.edu/Users/history/tucker/hh367/ButcheryattheBridge.htm (accessed May 20, 2006).

Vulliamy, Ed. *Seasons in Hell: Understanding Bosnia's War*. New York: St. Martin's Press, 1994.

Vulliamy, Ed. "The Warlord of Visegrad." *The Guardian* (August 11, 2005): www.guardian.co.uk/world/2005/aug/11/warcrimes.features11 (accessed May 20, 2006).

✦ INDEX